Grade 4

Increasing
Fluency
with
High Frequency Word Phrases

Directed by:
Edward Fry, Ph.D. and
Timothy Rasinski, Ph.D.

my last **penny**

the **powerful** beast

have remarkable **strength**

Author

Kathleen Knoblock

Editor
Jenni Corcoran, M.A.Ed.

Assistant Editor
Leslie Huber, M.A.

Editorial Director
Dona Herweck Rice

Editor-in-Chief
Sharon Coan, M.S.Ed.

Editorial Manager
Gisela Lee, M.A.

Creative Director
Lee Aucoin

Illustration Manager/Designer
Timothy J. Bradley

Imaging
Phil Garcia
Sandra Riley

Consultants
Edward Fry, Ph.D.
Timothy Rasinski, Ph.D.

Publisher
Corinne Burton, M.A.Ed.

Shell Education
5301 Oceanus Drive
Huntington Beach, CA 92649-1030
http://www.shelleducation.com
ISBN 978-1-4258-0279-0
© 2007 by Shell Educational Publishing, Inc.
Reprinted 2013

The classroom teacher may reproduce copies of materials in this book for classroom use only. The reproduction of any part for an entire school or school system is strictly prohibited. No part of this publication may be transmitted, stored, or recorded in any form without written permission from the publisher.

Table of Contents

Each lesson includes Fry Word Phrases, Story, Writing, Comprehension, Learning and Applying Prosody, Fluency Checkpoint, and Evaluation.

Phrasing for Fluency Lesson	Based on Fry's Level 4 Instant Words (1326–2025)	Reading with Expression (Prosody Skill Focus)	Page Number
Lesson 1	Instant Words 1326–1345	Pausing for Commas	page 13
Lesson 2	Instant Words 1346–1365	Commas + Chunked Phrases	page 17
Lesson 3	Instant Words 1366–1385	Using Volume for Stress	page 21
Lesson 4	Instant Words 1386–1405	Adjusting Pitch and Tone for Mood	page 25
Lesson 5	Instant Words 1406–1425	Author's Purpose	page 29
Lesson 6	Instant Words 1426–1445	Figures of Speech	page 33
Lesson 7	Instant Words 1446–1465	Using Stress to Support a Position	page 37
Lesson 8	Instant Words 1466–1485	Recognizing Point of View	page 41
Lesson 9	Instant Words 1486–1505	Chunk for Smoothness	page 45
Lesson 10	Instant Words 1506–1525	Tuning In to Final Punctuation	page 49
Lesson 11	Instant Words 1526–1565	Preparing for Surprises	page 53
Lesson 12	Instant Words 1566–1605	Getting the Rhythm	page 57
Lesson 13	Instant Words 1606–1645	Pronunciation for Accuracy	page 61
Lesson 14	Instant Words 1646–1685	Pitch and Volume	page 65
Lesson 15	Instant Words 1686–1745	Creating Suspense with Dialogue	page 69
Lesson 16	Instant Words 1746–1805	Audience	page 73
Lesson 17	Instant Words 1806–1845	Eye-Voice Span	page 77
Lesson 18	Instant Words 1846–1905	Signal Words and Phrases	page 81
Lesson 19	Instant Words 1906–1965	Showing Strong Feeling!	page 85
Lesson 20	Instant Words 1966–2025	Auto-Correct (Proofreading)	page 89

Standards Correlations

Shell Education is committed to producing educational materials that are research- and standards-based. In this effort, we have correlated all of our products to the academic standards of all 50 states, the District of Columbia, and the Department of Defense Dependent Schools. You can print a correlations report customized for your state directly from our website at **http://www.shelleducation.com.**

The No Child Left Behind legislation mandates that all states adopt academic standards that identify the skills students will learn in kindergarten through grade twelve. While many states had already adopted academic standards prior to NCLB, the legislation set requirements to ensure the standards were detailed and comprehensive.

Standards are designed to focus instruction and guide adoption of curricula. Standards are statements that describe the criteria necessary for students to meet specific academic goals. They define the knowledge, skills, and content students should acquire at each level. Standards are also used to develop standardized tests to evaluate students' academic progress.

In many states today, teachers are required to demonstrate how their lessons meet state standards. State standards are used in the development of all of our products, so educators can be assured they meet the academic requirements of each state.

To print a correlations report for this product, visit our website at **http://www.shelleducation. com** and follow the on-screen directions. If you require assistance in printing correlations reports, please contact Customer Service at (877) 777-3450.

McREL Compendium

Shell Education uses the Mid-continent Research for Education and Learning (McREL) Compendium to create standards correlations. Each year, McREL analyzes state standards and revises the compendium. By following this procedure, they are able to produce a general compilation of national standards.

The reading comprehension strategies assessed in this book are based on the following McREL content standards. All of the following standards apply to each lesson in this book.

1. The student previews text (e.g., skims material; uses pictures, textual clues, and text format).

2. The student establishes a purpose for reading (e.g., for information, for pleasure).

3. The student understands level-appropriate reading vocabulary (e.g., synonyms, antonyms, homophones, multi-meaning words).

4. The student reads aloud familiar stories, poems, and passages with fluency and expression (e.g., rhythm, flow, meter, tempo, pitch, tone, intonation).

5. The student adjusts speed of reading to suit purpose and difficulty of the material.

To see a state-specific correlation, visit the Shell Education website at **http://www.shelleducation.com.**

Introducing the Developers

Dr. Timothy Rasinski is a well-established authority in the fluency area of reading instruction. His many speaking appearances to teachers, as well as his landmark book, *The Fluent Reader* (Scholastic 2003), have introduced the concept of fluency to thousands of teachers.

Dr. Edward Fry has a decade-long association with a research-based, high-frequency list of words known as the Instant Words. He is also a frequent conference speaker and his most widely used book is *The Reading Teacher's Book of Lists* (Jossey Bass, 5th Edition, 2006).

Key themes of this grade-level book for classroom teachers come from elements of these two books: "chunking," or reading phrases as units, from Dr. Rasinski, and the rank ordering of the Instant Words from Dr. Fry.

Chunking is seen in the introductory phrases of each lesson where each phrase contains a grade-leveled Instant Word. Each of the phrases is also incorporated into a sample story in order to add meaning and improve fluency (Rasinski and Padak 1998).

The ordering of the Instant Words is important because it helps to answer the question, "Which words should I teach first, then next, etc.?" The answer comes from computer-based research that counts the frequency of millions of words in books, curriculum materials, and magazines (Carroll 1971, Sakiey 1977, Fry 2000).

Both Dr. Rasinski and Dr. Fry are indebted to Dr. Jay Samuels at the University of Minnesota, who is a real pioneer in the field of fluency. His article in the 1979 *Reading Teacher* titled "The Method of Repeated Reading" is regarded as a classic. Dr. Samuels has additional published research on the subject of fluency that has been a beneficial resource to those in the field (Samuels 2002).

The authors of this Shell Education series strongly agree that improving reading comprehension is important and that improved fluency contributes to improved comprehension. To further stress comprehension, each lesson contains a set of questions about elements such as main idea, details, vocabulary, and subjective or creative interpretations.

The authors further agree that this is not a "speed reading" course. While reading rate is an important aspect of fluency, so are the many elements of expression and prosody. Experienced teachers can tell a lot about a student's comprehension of a written passage by simply listening to him or her read aloud.

Professor Rasinski also has an interest in the use of reader's theater and poetry for repeated readings and, therefore, fluency development. Hence, in this book you will find the use of dialogue within the stories, as well as the use of poetry—all intended to enhance students' fluency development and enjoyment of learning.

Professor Fry is interested in the elements that make up prosody, such as pitch (high or low voice), punctuation, stress, pauses, and many others. These elements are partly based on *The Cambridge Encyclopedia of the English Language* by David Crystal.

How to Increase Fluency with High Frequency Word Phrases

Components and General Guidelines

On the road to becoming readers, students must not only learn to read and recognize words, but also recognize how combinations of words affect meaning. Although essential, word recognition and comprehension are not what make a reader fluent. To become fluent, students must also be able to read at a smooth pace and with appropriate expression. Can expression be taught? Yes! Students can be taught to use structural and contextual evidence in the writing as clues for how to read it. Students can also be taught strategies for recognizing mood, purpose, emotion, and other interpretive skills that they can then use to enhance expression. The lessons in this book target the three major components of fluency—accuracy, rate of reading, and expression.

However, no matter what or how much one tries to teach skills to students, one more critical component must be provided with regularity—the opportunity to hear fluent reading! The simple fact—that one must hear the language in order to become fluent in it—is frequently overlooked in the classroom. That is why this product provides not only activities in which students read, write, discuss, evaluate, and study written text, but also requires students to listen to text being read fluently. Included in this book is a CD that has the target phrases and the stories (or other text from each lesson) being read aloud with model fluency. Students can listen as often as necessary to both learn the words and phrases and also associate the written words and sentences in the passage with how it should sound.

The authors highly recommend that teachers frequently have students listen to model reading and also that each list of phrases and reading selections be read and reread aloud several times. Students need ample exposure to hearing model language and many opportunities to practice reading aloud themselves.

Materials Included in This Product

- 20 four-page lessons include Fry Word Phrases, stories or other text selections, writing, comprehension, learning and applying prosody, fluency checkpoint, and a student evaluation
- Fluency Assessment Rubric and reference list of oral reading fluency strategies
- Audio CD includes oral readings of the phrase lists and reading selections in each lesson
- Data CD includes copies of each reading selection for printing or making transparencies

Suggested Additional Materials

- A notebook or folder for each child to keep lesson materials and writing paper

© Shell Education

How to Use This Book

The Lessons—A Comprehensive Approach

This product combines two research-based approaches to teaching reading—**instant words** and **phrasing** (combining words into meaningful units). Together, these strategies are powerful tools for building fluency.

Many teachers of reading are familiar with Fry's Instant Words. These are words listed in order of frequency encountered in typical written material. The first 25 words make up about one-third of all printed material; the first 100, about half. Words 1–3000 listed have been roughly divided into six leveled lists in Dr. Fry's Spelling Book. Below is the breakdown by level:

Level 1: Instant Words 1–100	Level 4: Instant Words 1326–2025
Level 2: Instant Words 101–625	Level 5: Instant Words 2026–2725
Level 3: Instant Words 626–1325	Level 6: Instant Words 2726–3000

Dr. Fry's Spelling Book Levels 1–6: Words Most Needed Plus Phonics by Edward Fry, Ph.D.
© 1999, Teacher Created Materials, Inc.

The lessons in this book are based on Fry's Instant Words. Each lesson focuses on words from that level. Although not all words are used, the selected words are introduced sequentially. The lessons, therefore, should be done in order. Each lesson has the same eight components, described below.

Phrases

The instant words in the lesson are introduced in phrases that will appear in the story. These phrases are intended to be read aloud to students and practiced before they continue. The phrases should be reread as often as needed until students can read them "instantly."

Story

Each lesson has a story or other text selection for students to practice and read. When it is first presented, the phrases above appear in bold print in the story for easy recognition. Again, the story should be read aloud and reread as often as needed. In addition to the teacher reading, students can also listen to the story read with model fluency on the accompanying CD. In addition to listening to good model reading, students should be encouraged to practice and reread the material on their own, as well.

On Your Own

This section asks students to go back to the phrases or story and either identify certain types of phrases, use them in another way, or respond in writing to something about the story. This section serves the dual purpose of reviewing previous material and applying it in a different way and preparing for the next activity, comprehension.

Questions (Comprehension and Test Preparation)

Here, the student moves from literal reading of phrases and sentences to understanding what was read. The questions generally follow this sequential pattern: determining main idea; testing general comprehension (such as drawing conclusions, making inferences, identifying details, and recognizing fact and opinion); testing understanding of vocabulary and terms as used in the context of the story; and presenting one or more open-ended questions that target higher level, critical-thinking skills. This activity not only checks student comprehension, but also serves as test preparation and practice.

How to Use This Book (cont.)

Reading With Expression (Prosody Skill)

In each lesson, a specific skill related to reading with expression is presented. In some cases, it is a lesson on using structural and contextual evidence in the writing as clues to how it should be read. In others, the lesson focuses more on strategies for recognizing mood, purpose, emotion, and other interpretive skills, which students can use to enhance their oral communication and presentation. Although written "to the student," the lesson is intended to be read aloud to them by the teacher.

Try It!

Here, students have the opportunity to try the skill they have just learned. They have to apply it either to the story they read in the lesson or to new text. Students are encouraged to reread the story yet again. Directly following several of these activities is a "reminder" designed to summarize the skill and remind students to look for this skill in their current and future reading.

Fluency Checkpoint

Within each lesson is a fluency checkpoint, which suggests that students reread the passage as if they were rehearsing it for a performance, repeating this as many times as needed to be able to read it fluently. This can be done alone (whisper reading), in pairs, in a group, or with an aide, parent helper, or even a competent older student.

Evaluation

Finally, each lesson concludes with a student evaluation. Sometimes students will evaluate their own reading and fluency; other times, they are asked to evaluate each other. The purpose of this activity is to encourage students to reflect upon what they have done and to take ownership and responsibility for their own learning.

A Word About Reading Rate

Although the greater part of the lessons are devoted to accuracy, comprehension, and expression in oral reading, the rate of reading, or pace, is also a component of fluency. As students become more adept at reading through the other aspects of fluency, their rates of reading should continue to improve. Intermittently, but at least three times a year, do a formal fluency reading rate to check on each student. Make sure to use a passage in which the student has had opportunities to practice and rehearse both the text and the expression. Then, have him or her read it aloud for exactly one minute. Record the number of words the student reads accurately in one minute. Use this guide to determine general expectations for reading average, grade-level materials.

NUMBER OF WORDS READ CORRECTLY IN ONE MINUTE

Grade Level	First 1/3 of year	Middle of year	Last 1/3 of year
1		30	60
2	50	80	95
3	80	95	110
4	100	110	120
5	105	120	130
6	115	130	145

Adapted from *The Fluent Reader* by Timothy Rasinski, © 2003 Scholastic

 © Shell Education

How to Use This Book *(cont.)*

Pacing

With 20 lessons and about 36 weeks of school in a typical year, teachers do not need to feel rushed to complete a certain number of activities every week. Teachers can spread out the lessons by tailoring them to individual preferences. Keep in mind, though, that the lessons introduce words and phrases in sequential order, so it would best serve the students to teach them in this order.

Spend a little time each day, for at least a week, on pacing within a single lesson. The pacing plan that follows is just one suggestion.

Monday	• Distribute copies of the first page of the lesson. Read and reread the list of phrases. Talk about them. Do additional activities as needed. • Model reading the story with expression. Discuss it briefly and read it again. Allow students to practice reading the phrases and the story as much as necessary in order to read them with ease. • Make the CD readings available so students can listen to the readings of the phrases and the story. Keep this listening station open all week and encourage students to use it any time they have a few free moments.
Tuesday	• Distribute copies of the second page of the lesson. Read or have a student read the story aloud again. Read the directions for "On Your Own." If necessary, discuss further or do one or more examples together. Have students complete the activity. • Read the directions for the "Story Questions." Have students whisper-read the phrases and the story again. Then have students listen as you read the questions and choices aloud. Allow students time to mark their answers, including answering the open-ended question.
Wednesday	• Teach the lesson at the top of the third page by reading the explanation aloud to students and discussing the content. Give extra examples as needed. Ask students for examples to check their understanding of the skill. • Pass out copies of the third page of the lesson. If desired, have students follow along as you reread the lesson at the top. • Direct students' attention to the "Try It!" section. Read the directions and clarify as needed. Allow students time to complete the activity.
Thursday	• Give students time to reread and rehearse the passage as needed—alone, in pairs, in groups, or with a classroom helper. (The passage is repeated on the fourth page of the lesson, but without the phrases in bold.) This is an excellent time to do fluency checks—formally or informally. Listen to students read, or have them read to aides, parent helpers, or even competent older students. If a teacher has no assistance, he or she can choose at random several students to listen to each week. This way all students will be prepared, but the teacher only needs to check a few at a time. • While checking fluency or working with individual students, have the rest of the students complete the evaluation section of the lesson.
Friday	• Use this day to continue checking fluency and/or for reteaching and review. • Give students a follow-up assignment, such as drawing the setting of the story, writing a letter to the author, using a designated number of the underlined words in sentences, writing new phrases with the words, etc. • As students work independently, spend time with individuals or small groups of students who need additional support and practice.

How to Use This Book (cont.)

What About Differentiation?

Teachers can always extend or adapt lessons to meet their students' needs. Below are a few ideas for addressing different needs.

ELL (English Language Learners) and Others Who Need Extra Help With Language

Use the CD that accompanies this book to give students experiences with auditory-visual association, allowing them to make connections between the model reading on the CD and the text on the page. Have students use highlighters to mark certain things in the book, such as key words in the phrases, punctuation, stress, and figures of speech. To extend practice, make flash cards of the given phrases and then add other phrases, using the target instant words. For comprehension practice, play a game of "Catch Me If You Can." In this game, the teacher purposely misuses a word and the students try to "catch" the teacher's error. When reading the story or answering questions, pair students with helpers to give them that extra attention that may make the difference between trying again or giving up. When discussing stories, elicit from students ways that they can connect it to their real lives. Additional modifications include echo reading, having students create pictures (or other visual representations) of the phrases, and having students act out the phrases. Be patient, and encourage students to express their feelings and ask for help.

For Those Who Always Finish First and Those Who Get Bored Easily or Can Read Well Above Norms

First, children who excel in reading do not need to do the regular activity *plus* more. These students know busy work when they see it. Rather than give them additional work, a better approach is to give them alternate, challenging assignments from the start. For example, after reading the story, instead of the regular "On Your Own" activity, have these students do some more research on the topic, create a crossword puzzle from the instant words, write a different ending to the story, or write a different story in the same format using the same phrases from the list. These are just a few suggestions for differentiating the "On Your Own" activity, but each activity can be modified in a similar way. Choose activities, though, that have a purpose. In other words, require the students to report on their findings, use their crossword puzzles at a center, or read their original stories to the class.

A Note About Level 4

The selected reading passages vary in a number of ways. Some are fiction, some not. Some are longer and easier to read; others are shorter but more challenging. Throughout the lessons, the text reflects different writing genres. In addition to traditional stories and nonfiction text, there is at least one letter, poem, article, essay, and editorial. Note that Lessons 14, 16, 17, 18, and 20 are a little different from the rest. Lesson 14 converts a story into reader's theater. Lesson 16 is a whole-group lesson in which students participate in divided choral reading. Lessons 17–18 expose students to the five-paragraph essay format. Finally, Lesson 20 focuses on description and proofreading. Designed for the latter part of the year, these lessons should not only challenge your students to apply what they have learned, but also keep their attention right up to the last activity.

Techniques for Engaging Students in Oral Reading

Oral reading fosters fluency. Students need to hear model language in order to acquire it. Listening to good oral reading and participating in repeated reading strengthens accuracy, reading rate, and expression—the fundamentals of fluency. Here are a few ways to engage students in oral reading.

Oral Preview

Oral preview involves having students hear how the text should sound when it is read fluently, before they attempt to read it themselves. This strategy is especially helpful for students who are English Language Learners or who need more support. It is used in conjunction with other strategies and is the basis of every lesson in this book.

Repeated Reading

Repeated reading gives students a chance to "get to know" the text before being asked to read it aloud. The opportunity to practice increases both willingness and proficiency with regard to oral reading. This technique is highly recommended for students as they do the lessons in this book.

Paired Reading

This strategy involves two readers sharing the presentation of the text. Paired reading can include two students, a student and an adult, a student and an older student, or a student and a teacher. In its best form, paired reading involves a more proficient reader paired with a less proficient one, so that the stronger one can support the other.

Call and Response/Refrain

Call and response is a type of choral reading. One student reads a portion of a text and then the class or a small group responds by reading the next portion in unison. When the response portion is a repetition of the same text, it is called a refrain.

Divided Reading

In this version of choral reading, assigned sections of the text are read by groups of students.

Reader's Theater

In reader's theater, the text is read like a script. It is like a play, but with some important differences. Although the students practice for the "performance," they read, rather than memorize, their lines. Students may use simple props, but there are no costumes, sets, or "action." The script may have a few parts, many parts, and even parts that are read by all participants.

A Three-Component Rubric for Assessing Fluency

Assessing Fluency

At first, one might think that assessing fluency might only produce vague, subjective descriptions, such as "he reads well," "she reads with no expression," and so on. The goal is for students to become fluent, but fluency is not measurable by objective standards. Although fluency can't be measured with a right or wrong score, it can be assessed more accurately by using the rubric below.

Score	Accuracy	Rate (Pace)	Expression	
			Structural paraphrasing, pausing. smoothness, pitch, volume	**Interpretive** mood, purpose, emotion, subtleties of meaning
4	Recognizes most words and reads them correctly without hesitation.	Consistently reads at natural, conversational pace, or as appropriate for the text.	Reads smoothly. Consistently uses meaningful phrasing and appropriate pausing. Adjusts pitch and volume to the circumstances (type of text or audience).	Recognizes different purposes for reading. Consistently conveys the appropriate mood and emotion. Distinguishes word meanings in context.
3	Recognizes pre-taught and familiar words and reads them correctly. May hesitate, but can use context and apply word attack skills.	Sometimes reads at a conversational pace, but is inconsistent. May speed up and slow down or generally read at a slightly slower pace.	Reads smoothly in general, but with some breaks or misuse of pausing. Is aware of pitch and volume.	Reads most text with emphasis appropriate for the purpose and mood of the text. May at times slip into concentrating on pronunciation, but will usually recover and resume once past the problematic area.
2	Recognizes and reads some words correctly, but hesitates. Has some difficulty using context clues and applying word attack skills.	Reads somewhat slower than appropriate for text. May have stops and starts or have to go back and reread.	Reads unevenly. May miss punctuation clues resulting in choppiness or run-on reading. Does not generally attend to pitch and volume.	May use natural-sounding language at times, but, in general, frequently resorts to focusing on word-by-word pronunciation without regard for the mood, purpose, or intended meaning.
1	Misreads words frequently. May not recognize words in different contexts. Is not adept at applying word attack skills.	Reading is slow and laborious. Frequently hesitates, stops, or goes back to "start over."	Does not usually read in meaningful units, such as phrases or clauses. May read word-for-word with little attention to context or punctuation signals.	Reading is generally monotone and lacks a sense of awareness of mood, purpose, or emotion. May not recognize word meanings in context.

Throughout this book, fluency is described as the ability to read with accuracy, with expression, and at a good pace. Note in the chart above that expression has been subdivided. For the purposes of evaluation and scoring, it may be useful to rate expression based on structural factors and interpretation separately. To record a single expression score, combine the two subcategory scores.

Possible scores range from **4** (lowest) to **16** (highest). Generally, a total score of **8** or above suggests that a student is progressing in fluency. A score below **8** may indicate that fluency is a concern.

© Shell Education

Name _____ Date _____

Phrases

Read these phrases to yourself as you listen to them being read aloud.

a real <u>Texas</u> longhorn	in <u>Texas</u>	from the <u>Atlantic</u> to the <u>Pacific</u>
tall-tale <u>characters</u>	shared their <u>breakfast</u>	their <u>prime</u> meat
had to <u>hurry</u>	the <u>secret</u> got out	the cowboys were <u>concerned</u>
<u>everybody</u> knew	paid his <u>dues</u>	

Could you read every word? If not, repeat reading and listening until you can. Then, try reading the phrases on your own without listening.

Story

Read the story to yourself as you listen to it being read aloud. Repeat reading and listening until you know every word.

Have you heard of Paul Bunyan and his blue ox? They are make-believe **tall-tale characters**. However, there is another famous "Blue" who was **a real Texas longhorn** steer.

The Texas Longhorn is a symbol of the Old West. It is named for its horns, which can stretch six feet across. These tough creatures adjusted well to life on the range. Cattle were driven north to feed on the open grasslands. Later, **their prime meat** was sold in cities **from the Atlantic to the Pacific**. However, even with established trails, the cowboys had a hard time keeping the huge herds controlled and moving.

In the 1870s, a man named Charles Goodnight had a cattle ranch **in Texas**. His lead steer was a 1400-pound longhorn named "Old Blue." This gentle giant seemed to have a talent for leading the herds. Sometimes the cowboys **had to hurry** just to keep up! Over time, **the secret got out.** Soon, **everybody knew** about Old Blue. As far as **the cowboys were concerned**, Old Blue was almost one of the boys. On trips he slept near the cowboys. They even **shared their breakfast** with him. In his eight years as lead longhorn, Old Blue led more than 10,000 cattle. After he retired, everyone figured that he'd **paid his dues**. He lived out his life on Charles Goodnight's ranch, pampered and fed like a beloved pet.

Lesson 1 *(cont.)*

Name _____ Date _____

On Your Own

Look again at the bold phrases in the story. Then, choose and write the one that best completes each sentence below.

1. Paul Bunyan and his blue ox are make-believe _____ .
2. Cattle were sold for meat in cities _____ .
3. Charles Goodnight had a cattle ranch _____ .
4. When Old Blue retired, everyone figured that he'd _____ .

Story Questions Main Idea, Cause & Effect, Vocabulary, Critical Thinking

Think about the story you listened to and practiced on page 13. Now, find out how well you understood it! Answer the questions below. You may need to go back and read the story again.

1. Which of these would be the best title for this story?

   A. Paul Bunyan and His Blue Ox

   B. The Old West

   C. Charles Goodnight's Ranch

   D. A Texas Longhorn Legend

2. Old Blue can be described as *quite a character.* What does that mean?

   A. Old Blue was a fictional character in a story.

   B. Old Blue has unusual character traits for a longhorn.

   C. Old Blue has human characteristics.

   D. All of the above.

3. How is the word *steer* used in this story?

   A. as a noun meaning male cattle

   B. as a verb meaning to guide in a certain direction

   C. both A and B

   D. neither A nor B

4. Sometimes stories tell you things directly. Other times you have to figure out things from clues in the story. Even though the story doesn't say so, why do you think the famous Texas longhorn was named *Old Blue?*

   _____

   _____

   _____

   _____

Name _____ Date _____

 # Reading with Expression—Pausing for Commas

A sentence is a complete thought that ends with a period, question mark, or exclamation point. You already know that these marks are signals to stop. However, sometimes sentences are long. Does it ever seem that all the words run together and that you are lost by the time you get to the end? In order to read and understand a long sentence, such as this one, short pauses are needed to break it up. That is one of the important jobs of a little punctuation mark called a comma (,). Good writers use commas to signal a short pause in a sentence. Although commas are small, they are powerful helpers when reading. Let's take a look at a few sentences from the story.

Here is a long sentence from the story with the commas taken out. Try to read it straight through without pausing.

Even with established trails the cowboys had a hard time keeping the huge herds controlled and moving.

Did your tongue get a little tied up? Now read it again, this time pausing just for a split second at the comma.

Even with established trails, the cowboys had a hard time keeping the huge herds controlled and moving.

What a difference that little comma makes! Just a little pause at a comma helps you better express the meaning of the sentence and makes your reading clearer and easier to understand.

Try It!

Practice paying special attention to those little, but powerful, commas. Each of these sentences is missing a comma. Find and reread the sentence in the story. Then insert the comma (,) where it belongs in the sentences below.

1. It is named for its horns which can stretch six feet across.
2. In the 1870s a man named Charles Goodnight had a cattle ranch in Texas.
3. As far as the cowboys were concerned Old Blue was almost one of the boys.
4. In his eight years as lead longhorn Old Blue led more than 10,000 cattle.
5. He lived out his life on Charles Goodnight's ranch pampered and fed like a beloved pet.

 The next time you read this or another story, pay special attention to the commas. They are signals that tell you to pause for just a split second, but that split second makes a big difference in how well you read and understand sentences.

Name _____ Date _____

 ## Fluency Checkpoint

You have already listened to, practiced, and read the story below. Now it's time to check your reading fluency. Remember, fluency means not just getting the words right, but also reading at a good rate and with expression, or feeling. Reread the story again, as if you were rehearsing it for a performance. Repeat this as many times as necessary so that you can read it fluently.

Have you heard of Paul Bunyan and his blue ox? They are make-believe tall-tale characters. However, there is another famous "Blue" who was a real Texas longhorn steer.

The Texas Longhorn is a symbol of the Old West. It is named for its horns, which can stretch six feet across. These tough creatures adjusted well to life on the range. Cattle were driven north to feed on the open grasslands. Later, their prime meat was sold in cities from the Atlantic to the Pacific. However, even with established trails, the cowboys had a hard time keeping the huge herds controlled and moving.

In the 1870s, a man named Charles Goodnight had a cattle ranch in Texas. His lead steer was a 1400-pound longhorn named "Old Blue." This gentle giant seemed to have a talent for leading the herds. Sometimes the cowboys had to hurry just to keep up! Over time, the secret got out. Soon, everybody knew about Old Blue. As far as the cowboys were concerned, Old Blue was almost one of the boys. On trips he slept near the cowboys. They even shared their breakfast with him. In his eight years as lead longhorn, Old Blue led more than 10,000 cattle. After he retired, everyone figured that he'd paid his dues. He lived out his life on Charles Goodnight's ranch, pampered and fed like a beloved pet.

Evaluation

Looking back, how well do *you* think you did with each part of the lesson? Underline the phrase that best expresses your opinion.

Reading the phrases?	*very well*	*could be better*	*not as well as I'd like*
Understanding the story?	*very well*	*could be better*	*not as well as I'd like*
Using punctuation for expression?	*very well*	*could be better*	*not as well as I'd like*
Reading rate?	*very well*	*could be better*	*not as well as I'd like*

© Shell Education

Name _____ Date _____

Phrases

Read these phrases to yourself as you listen to them being read aloud.

roar the news out loud

what this wonder consists of

would be no peace

through the dust

my brain was racing

a young fellow

whispered to myself

in Egypt

we could establish

held my breath

my last penny

the gate that opens

of an officer or guard

Could you read every word? If not, repeat reading and listening until you can. Then, try reading the phrases on your own without listening.

Story

Read the story to yourself as you listen to it being read aloud. Repeat reading and listening until you know every word.

Journal of Howard Carter   *Egypt, November 4, 1922*

For five years, Lord Carnarvon and I searched in vain. Now I have been digging **in Egypt** again. Not long ago when my funding ran out, I vowed to continue looking in the Valley of Kings for Tut's tomb, even if it took **my last penny**. Although Lord Carnarvon has not returned with me, he did agree to fund the search for one more year.

Three days ago, **a young fellow** came to me saying that he had seen a step cut into the rock under some workmen's huts. I **held my breath** and thought, "Could this be **the gate that opens** to a yet undiscovered tomb of a king?"

Quickly, I ordered the men to clear away the sand. It was not long before **we could establish** that there were eleven more steps. Then, **through the dust**, I could see a door. I recognized the seal **of an officer or guard** on the door.

My brain was racing. There **would be no peace** until I knew what was behind that door. I made a small hole and peeked inside. As I looked through the tiny opening, I wanted to **roar the news out loud**, but instead held my tongue and just **whispered to myself**, "At last I have made a wonderful discovery."

Tonight I can hardly control my excitement. But before I see **what this wonder consists of**, I must telegram Lord Carnarvon in England with the news. He will want to be here for the grand entry.

Footnote: *Lord Carnarvon arrived in three weeks. On November 26, they opened the chamber of King Tut's tomb.*

Lesson 2 *(cont.)*

Name _____ Date _____

On Your Own

Find and write the bold phrase from the story that tells

1. **where** Howard Carter was digging: _____
2. **who** told Carter about the step cut into the rock: _____
3. **how** Carter spoke the news: _____
4. **where** Carter saw a door: _____

Story Questions Main Idea, Details, Vocabulary, Critical Thinking

Think about the story you listened to and practiced on page 17. Now, find out how well you understood it! Answer the questions below. You may need to go back and read the story again.

1. Which best tells what the whole story is about, or its main idea?
   A. King Tut was buried in the Valley of the Kings.
   B. In 1922, Howard Carter discovered the tomb of King Tut.
   C. A young fellow, not Howard Carter, discovered the location of the tomb.
   D. Howard Carter waited for Lord Carnarvon to arrive before opening the tomb.

2. Number these statements 1–5 to show the order in which the events happened.
   _____ Carter returned alone and was led to a step under some workmen's huts.
   _____ Carter telegrammed the news to Carnarvon and said to join him.
   _____ Carter and Carnarvon searched together for Tut's tomb.
   _____ Carter opened the door to the chamber of King Tut's tomb.
   _____ Carter peeked through a small hole in the door to see what was inside.

3. In which sentence does *establish* have the same meaning as it did in the story?
   A. The Great Pyramid is an established wonder of the world. (*fixed permanently*)
   B. This would establish Carter's name as the discoverer of Tut's tomb. (*recognized*)
   C. They need to establish a camp near the dig site. (*set up or start*)
   D. It was hard to establish where the entrance would be found. (*prove or confirm*)

4. The story tells of an important discovery made by Howard Carter in 1922. Do you think that this is the actual journal of Howard Carter written in 1922, or just an interesting way for the author to present the historical facts? Write your answer and at least one reason you think as you do.

   _____

   _____

   _____

Name _____ Date _____

Reading with Expression—Commas + Chunked Phrases

Imagine that you were given a big candy bar. Would you try to stuff it in your mouth all at once? No, you would eat it in bites, or chunks. That way, you can chew a little bit at a time and enjoy it without choking by trying to swallow it whole.

You can think of reading sentences and even paragraphs like eating a candy bar. If you break up the words into chunks, it is easier to understand and swallow the whole idea!

The trick is to look for natural breaks in the words. It is not as hard as you might think. Sometimes there are commas to split sentences into chunks. Look at how the commas help you read this sentence:

In the chamber they found King Tut's mummy, cooking utensils, and golden treasures.

Now read the same sentence with the commas misplaced.

In the chamber they found King Tut's mummy cooking, utensils, and golden treasures.

Carter was surprised to find the chamber. Imagine if he found King Tut's mummy cooking!

Even with commas there to split chunks for you, sometimes you have to break a sentence down even further by looking for other groups of words, or phrases, that make sense together. Here's an example of a long sentence from the story. Pause at the commas, of course, and also just a tiny bit at the end of each chunked phrase (/).

> Not long ago / when my funding ran out, I vowed to continue looking /
> in the Valley of Kings / for Tut's tomb, even if it took / my last penny.

Try It!

Now, try choosing the correct chunking to break up sentences into small meaningful parts. Each sentence is chunked two different ways. Read them with small pauses at the end of each chunk. Then underline the sentence in each pair that shows the correct, meaningful chunks.

1. A. During the nap / he took the bite of a mosquito / on his / nose woke him up.

   B. During the nap he took / the bite of a mosquito on his nose / woke him up.

2. A. For lunch / the workers had bread / cheese cookies / and milk.

   B. For lunch / the workers had bread / cheese / cookies / and milk.

3. A. Lord Carvarnon, I've found the door / steps / and a royal burial chamber.

   B. Lord / Carvarnon I've found the / door steps / and a royal burial / chamber.

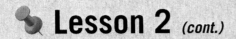

Name _____ Date _____

 # Fluency Checkpoint

You have already listened to, practiced, and read the story below. Now it's time to check your reading fluency. Remember, fluency means not just getting the words right, but also reading at a good rate and with expression, or feeling. Reread the story again, as if you were rehearsing it for a performance. Repeat this as many times as necessary so that you can read it fluently.

Journal of Howard Carter   *Egypt, November 4, 1922*

For five years, Lord Carnarvon and I searched in vain. Now, I have been digging in Egypt again. Not long ago when my funding ran out, I vowed to continue looking in the Valley of Kings for Tut's tomb, even if it took my last penny. Although Lord Carnarvon has not returned with me, he did agree to fund the search for one more year.

Three days ago, a young fellow came to me saying that he had seen a step cut into the rock under some workmen's huts. I held my breath and thought, "Could this be the gate that opens to a yet undiscovered tomb of a king?"

Quickly, I ordered the men to clear away the sand. It was not long before we could establish that there were eleven more steps. Then, through the dust, I could see a door. I recognized the seal of an officer or guard on the door.

My brain was racing. There would be no peace until I knew what was behind that door. I made a small hole and peeked inside. As I looked through the tiny opening, I wanted to roar the news out loud, but instead held my tongue and just whispered to myself, "At last I have made a wonderful discovery."

Tonight I can hardly control my excitement. But before I see what this wonder consists of, I must telegram Lord Carnarvon in England with the news. He will want to be here for the grand entry.

Footnote: *Lord Carnarvon arrived in three weeks. On November 26, they opened the chamber of King Tut's tomb.*

Evaluation

Think back over this whole lesson. What was the easiest part? The hardest? Look at the list below. Then, use the numbers 1 through 5 to rate them—with 1 being the easiest to 5 being the hardest.

_____ Reading the words and phrases

_____ Understanding the story

_____ Answering the story questions

_____ Understanding chunking

_____ Reading with fluency (speed, accuracy, and expression)

Name _____ Date _____

Phrases

Read these phrases to yourself as you listen to them being read aloud.

at the <u>pond</u>

made of hydrogen and <u>carbon</u>

used in this <u>manner</u>

<u>disappeared</u> below the surface

something more <u>serious</u>

<u>floating</u> back and forth

<u>scientific</u> experiment

packed up a <u>lunch</u>

how to <u>improve</u>

they <u>approached</u>

Could you read every word? If not, repeat reading and listening until you can. Then, try reading the phrases on your own without listening.

Story

Read the story to yourself as you listen to it being read aloud. Repeat reading and listening until you know every word.

One afternoon my mom thought it would be fun to take my little sisters to feed the ducks **at the pond** in the park. She **packed up a lunch** and off we went.

She was right about my little sisters. They were having fun. I was bored. I just sat there watching the ducks **floating back and forth**. **They approached** my sisters quacking. When the bread they threw started to sink, the ducks' heads **disappeared below the surface**, then popped back up. My sisters were delighted, but I had to think about **something more serious**—my science homework that wasn't getting done. I had to come up with an experiment. It had to be something that demonstrates **how to improve** something in real life.

While watching the ducks, my mind drifted to thoughts about the birds and other animals that have been caught in oil spills. Because oil and water don't mix, the oil floats on the top. The animals get coated in it. How do you clean up oil? That was it! My **scientific experiment** would be testing ways to remove oil from water.

Later, at home, I found a simple experiment to do just that. The instructions said to test how well each of these things removed vegetable oil poured into a bowl of water: fish net, gauze, and something called *polypropylene* cloth. (This is a fancy name for a material used as a liner in socks and gloves. I got some at a sports store.)

Of course, when I did the experiment, the polypropylene worked best. After some research I figured out why. Polypropylene and oil are both **made of hydrogen and carbon**, so they both float. The polypropylene floats on the oil and absorbs it. When **used in this manner** on oil spills, the polypropylene easily picks up and removes the oil.

By the way, my sisters had a good time **at the pond**. I not only got an *A* on my experiment, but I learned something important, too.

Name _____ Date _____

On Your Own

Below are six phrases from the story. Beside each, write a phrase using the underlined word a different way. The first one is done for you to show you how.

1. at the <u>pond</u>   _____ near the pond _____
2. something more <u>serious</u> _____
3. <u>floating</u> back and forth _____
4. how to <u>improve</u> _____
5. <u>scientific</u> experiment _____
6. <u>disappeared</u> below the surface _____

Story Questions   Main Idea, Details, Vocabulary, Critical Thinking

Think about the story you listened to and practiced on page 21. Now, find out how well you understood it! Answer the questions below. You may need to go back and read the story again.

1. Which of these would be the best title for this story?
    A. Lunch in the Park
    B. Delightful Ducks
    C. From Bored to Inspired
    D. Doing My Science Homework

2. What is the question to be answered by the experiment?
    A. How do you clean up oil from water?
    B. How do oil spills happen?
    C. What effect does an oil spill have on birds?
    D. Why do ducks float instead of sinking?

3. What is *polypropylene* and what does it have in common with oil?

    _____

    _____

    _____

4. Why does the writer begin the fifth paragraph with the words *Of course*?
    A. The writer knew that the polypropylene would work best before doing the experiment.
    B. The writer didn't actually do the experiment.
    C. The writer had already told the readers what polypropylene was.
    D. The writer already knew why polypropylene is used on oil spills.

Name _____ Date _____

Reading with Expression—Using Volume for Stress

Reading out loud is more than just knowing and saying the words. If that were true, we would all sound like robots. Try reading this sentence like a robot: **Wow. That was exciting.** Something is missing. A robot does not have feelings, and so the sentence does not show any feeling. However, people do have feelings, and they use their voices to express them. One way we do this is by saying words or parts of words louder and stronger than other parts. We do this because we want to stress something about what we are saying. Sometimes the whole meaning of a sentence can change by just stressing different parts of it. In the sentence below, read the part that is underlined a little louder and stronger. Then, see how the meaning changes.

I was <u>bored</u>.   I <u>was</u> bored.   <u>I</u> was bored.

Now, answer these questions out loud with one of the sentences. Choose the one that shows the correct stress. 1. What were you feeling? 2. Were you bored? 3. Who was bored?

In a story, how do you know which way to read it? In other words, how do you know what word to stress? You have to be aware of the feelings of the characters or the writer at the moment. Often the sentences will give you clues. For example, in the story about lunch at the park, look at what comes right before the sentence *I was bored*. Stress the underlined words. Then, for the sentence *I was bored*, try stressing all three words one at a time. Underline the one word that should be stressed.

She was right about my <u>sisters</u>. <u>They</u> were having fun. I was bored.

Try It!

Now, try figuring out what word to stress in these sentences. Use the clues to decide which word to underline in each quote. Test your answer by whisper reading with the underlined word stressed (said a little bit louder and stronger).

1. I wanted to be home getting my homework done. "What am I doing here?" I asked myself.
2. I thought about all the poor animals caught in oil spills. "Can't anything be done to prevent this?" I thought sadly.
3. We can't prevent oil spills, but I read about a material that quickly picks up oil spilled in water. "The oil spills may still happen, but at least there is something that can clean it up!"

The next time you read a story, pay special attention to the feelings that the words are supposed to express. Make your voice a little louder and stronger to stress important words.

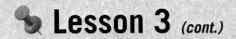

Name _____ Date _____

 Fluency Checkpoint

You have already listened to, practiced, and read the story below. Now it's time to check your reading fluency. Remember, fluency means not just getting the words right, but also reading at a good rate and with expression, or feeling. Reread the story again, as if you were rehearsing it for a performance. Repeat this as many times as necessary so that you can read it fluently.

One afternoon my mom thought it would be fun to take my little sisters to feed the ducks at the pond in the park. She packed up a lunch and off we went.

She was right about my little sisters. They were having fun. I was bored. I just sat there watching the ducks floating back and forth. They approached my sisters quacking. When the bread they threw started to sink, the ducks' heads disappeared below the surface, then popped back up. My sisters were delighted, but I had to think about something more serious—my science homework that wasn't getting done. I had to come up with an experiment. It had to be something that demonstrates how to improve something in real life.

While watching the ducks, my mind drifted to thoughts about the birds and other animals that have been caught in oil spills. Because oil and water don't mix, the oil floats on the top. The animals get coated in it. How do you clean up oil? That was it! My scientific experiment would be testing ways to remove oil from water.

Later, at home, I found a simple experiment to do just that. The instructions said to test how well each of these things removed vegetable oil poured into a bowl of water: fish net, gauze, and something called *polypropylene* cloth. (This is a fancy name for a material used as a liner in socks and gloves. I got some at a sports store.)

Of course, when I did the experiment, the polypropylene worked best. After some research I figured out why. Polypropylene and oil are both made of hydrogen and carbon, so they both float. The polypropylene floats on the oil and absorbs it. When used in this manner on oil spills, the polypropylene easily picks up and removes the oil.

By the way, my sisters had a good time at the pond. I not only got an *A* on my experiment, but I learned something important, too.

Evaluation

Work in a group of three to evaluate this lesson. First, compare your answers in the "Try It" section. Each of you read your answer, stressing the word you underlined. Then, read it stressing different words. Decide together which is the best way to express the answer.

Next, go back to the story. There are six paragraphs. Take turns reading two paragraphs each aloud while the others listen. At the end of the story, evaluate your skill at stressing important words.

Check one box ☑. ☐ My skill at stressing important words is good.

☐ My skill at stressing important words is coming along.

☐ Whoops. I forgot to do that.

Name _____ Date _____

Phrases

Read these phrases to yourself as you listen to them being read aloud.

firmly planted	his skin was rough	explore the world
a skilled artist	drew, painted, and carved	a scene of Inuit men
in Alaska	wooden and ivory carvings	of the old tribes
the powerful beast	as is standard	
the future is yours	for future generations	

Could you read every word? If not, repeat reading and listening until you can. Then, try reading the phrases on your own without listening.

Story

Read the story to yourself as you listen to it being read aloud. Repeat reading and listening until you know every word.

Lucy grew up **in Alaska**. **As is standard** in Inuit tradition, the whole family lived under one roof. As the oldest, Great Grandpa had a place of honor.

"GG," as Lucy fondly called him, was very old—no one quite knew how old. **His skin was rough**, but his eyes were soft. When he told tales **of the old tribes**, everyone listened. Although modern, the house was filled with his Inuit history.

Like many Inuit, GG was **a skilled artist.** He **drew, painted, and carved** his memories to save **for future generations**. **A scene of Inuit men** on a hunt for caribou hung on the wall. Above the door was a three-foot-long walrus tusk that GG had polished to a shine. **Firmly planted** on the mantle were **wooden and ivory carvings** that GG had crafted by hand. A real polar bear skin was spread across his bed. GG claimed to have brought **the powerful beast** down himself!

The spring before Lucy went off to college—the first in her family to do so—she sat with old Great Grandpa. "Go **explore the world**, my dear. **The future is yours,**" he said. "But never forget your people." That fall, while Lucy was away, Great Grandpa passed on.

Lucy never forgot. She later told her own children about their Great *Great* Grandpa. She passed on her proud heritage as an Inuit—a word meaning "the people" in Inupiaq, GG's native language.

 # Lesson 4 *(cont.)*

Name _____ Date _____

On Your Own

Read through the story. Find a bold word in the story that belongs in each sentence below.

1. Great Grandpa was a skilled _____ who drew, painted, and made carvings.
2. A polar bear is a big and _____ beast.
3. On the wall hung a _____ of Inuit men on a hunt for caribou.
4. Great Grandpa had _____ skin, but soft eyes.
5. It is a _____ Inuit tradition for the whole family to live in one house.

Story Questions Main Idea, Drawing Conclusions, Vocabulary, Critical Thinking

Think about the story you listened to and practiced on page 25. Now, find out how well you understood it! Answer the questions below. You may need to go back and read the story again.

1. Which best tells what the whole story is about, or its main idea?
   A. Listening to older people is important.
   B. Going to college is the only way to explore the world.
   C. The old ways of doing things are better than new ways.
   D. Heritage is passed down from generation to generation.

2. Which of the following are animals that live in Alaska?
   A. walrus
   B. polar bear
   C. caribou
   D. All of the above.

3. The phrase *passed on* is used with two different meanings in the story. Which two?
   A. *went* by and *skipped*
   B. *died* and *continued*
   C. *went* by and *continued*
   D. *died* and *skipped*

4. Sometimes a phrase means something other than what the words actually say. Write what each of these sentences really means.
   A. The house was filled with Inuit history. _____

   _____

   B. Carvings were firmly planted on the mantle. _____

   _____

   C. Great Grandpa carved his memories in ivory and wood. _____

   _____

#50279—Increasing Fluency with High Frequency Word Phrases   © *Shell Education*

Name _____ Date _____

Reading with Expression—Adjusting Pitch and Tone for Mood

Everyone who has feelings has moods. Unlike a specific feeling, such as amusement or anger, a mood is a general, overall state of feeling, such as being suspicious or relaxed. Usually when we are in a good or bad mood, it is because of a collection of feelings or things that have happened to make us feel that way. You may be in a happy mood because you had a good dinner, got your homework done, and your best friend called. You may be in a bad mood because your mom is mad at you, it's too hot, and you can't find your library book. So, a person's mood depends on how that person feels and what recent experiences he or she has had. An important thing to remember about moods is that they are temporary—they don't last a long time and can change often when circumstances change.

Stories have moods, too. For example, if you read a story about a haunted castle, the mood will be eerie. On the other hand, if you read a story about a kid who turns into a mouse, the mood will be silly. Of course, just as you express yourself differently when you are in different moods, when you read a story, you want to express the mood of the story and the characters in it. How? Just like you do when you are talking. You would read about a haunted castle in a slow, low voice. You would read about the kid-turned-mouse quicker and in a higher voice. Just like our moods, though, sometimes the mood of the story changes quickly as events unfold. As a reader, you need to learn to recognize mood in a story and when it changes.

Try It!

Now, try recognizing the mood in what you are reading. First, read each section silently and then out loud in a whisper voice. Answer the question about the mood. Then, write whether you would read it aloud in a slow, low voice, or in a quicker, higher voice.

1. Today just seems so long. It's like the clock is ticking slower and slower. Will this day—this hour—ever end?

   Which describes the mood—content or bored? _____

   How would you read it aloud? _____

2. The tiny man wagged his finger at me. "Hey, watch your step, big boy!"

   Which describes the mood—light-hearted or weary? _____

   How would you read it aloud? _____

3. My whole life I have listened to Great Grandpa tell stories about our people and the old ways. Now that he is gone, all I have of him are my memories.

   Which describes the mood—amusing or painful? _____

   How would you read it aloud? _____

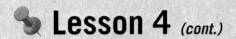

Name _____ Date _____

 ## Fluency Checkpoint

You have already listened to, practiced, and read the story below. Now it's time to check your reading fluency. Remember, fluency means not just getting the words right, but also reading at a good rate and with expression, or feeling. Reread the story again, as if you were rehearsing it for a performance. Repeat this as many times as necessary so that you can read it fluently.

Lucy grew up in Alaska. As is standard in Inuit tradition, the whole family lived under one roof. As the oldest, Great Grandpa had a place of honor.

"GG," as Lucy fondly called him, was very old—no one quite knew how old. His skin was rough, but his eyes were soft. When he told tales of the old tribes, everyone listened. Although modern, the house was filled with his Inuit history.

Like many Inuit, GG was a skilled artist. He drew, painted, and carved his memories to save for future generations. A scene of Inuit men on a hunt for caribou hung on the wall. Above the door was a three-foot-long walrus tusk that GG had polished to a shine. Firmly planted on the mantle were wooden and ivory carvings that GG had crafted by hand. A real polar bear skin was spread across his bed. GG claimed to have brought the powerful beast down himself!

The spring before Lucy went off to college—the first in her family to do so—she sat with old Great Grandpa. "Go explore the world, my dear. The future is yours," he said. "But never forget your people." That fall, while Lucy was away, Great Grandpa passed on.

Lucy never forgot. She later told her own children about their Great *Great* Grandpa. She passed on her proud heritage as an Inuit—a word meaning "the people" in Inupiaq, GG's native language.

Evaluation

Think back over this whole lesson. Read the story aloud one more time. Then, complete each sentence with the phrase that tells how you think you read.

1. I think my rate of reading was _____
   (too slow, too fast, just right)

2. When I read the story, I _____
   (stumbled on words, forgot words, got the words right)

3. I _____ to use my voice to express the mood.
   (remembered, didn't remember, sometimes remembered)

Name _____ Date _____

Phrases

Read these phrases to yourself as you listen to them being read aloud.

can they <u>identify</u>	if an <u>individual</u>	will be the <u>date</u>
a <u>desk</u> job	<u>relative</u> of mine	to start <u>immediately</u>
a little <u>spirit</u>	have remarkable <u>strength</u>	push a <u>button</u>
in the police <u>library</u>	have an <u>effect</u>	

Could you read every word? If not, repeat reading and listening until you can. Then, try reading the phrases on your own without listening.

Story

Read the story to yourself as you listen to it being read aloud. Repeat reading and listening until you know every word.

I am a cop on the Super Powers Police Force (SPPF). I have been on the job stopping villains for a long time. Things are just not the way they used to be when I was a young superhero. These days it seems that all kids think that they **have remarkable strength** or special powers. It is not as if you can just **push a button** and suddenly become a superhero. Well, most of the time anyway. There was this **relative of mine**, who could just **push a button** on his sleeve and. . . Never mind. That's another story.

As I was saying, today it seems like there are more heroes than there are criminals to catch! The force will accept just about anyone with even the smallest super ability. **Can they identify if an individual** even has a superpower anymore? These young "heroes" come in and expect **to start immediately**. They are so full of themselves. They think they can just skip the training and go right out on the street! Poof! Criminals caught! Just like that! I say, **a little spirit** and a name such as "Dee Terrent" does not a superhero make!

Perhaps you are wondering why I would not be glad that there are so many young men and women joining the SPPF. It's pretty simple. Next week **will be the date** of my 25th anniversary with the force. Although I still think I can **have an effect** on the bad guys who roam the streets, my boss feels differently. Tomorrow, I am being moved to **a desk job in the police library**. What scoundrels am I supposed to catch there? Flies?

Lesson 5 (cont.)

Name _____ Date _____

On Your Own

Some phrases tell when, where, or why. Others show action. The phrases below are verb phrases, meaning they show action. First, underline the action word, or verb, in the phrase. Then, go back and find it in the story. On the line in front of each phrase, identify *who* in the story is doing the action.

1. _____ have remarkable strength
2. _____ could push a button on his sleeve
3. _____ accept just about anyone
4. _____ expect to start immediately
5. _____ have an effect on the bad guys

Story Questions Main Idea, Details, Vocabulary, Critical Thinking

Think about the story you listened to and practiced on page 29. Now, find out how well you understood it! Answer the questions below. You may need to go back and read the story again.

1. Which best tells what the whole story is about, or its main idea?

   A. Just because someone is older doesn't mean that he or she can no longer do a job.

   B. Young superheroes are stronger than older ones.

   C. Some older people don't like younger ones and can be jealous of them.

   D. After doing a job for 25 years, a person doesn't have to work hard anymore.

2. Which of these pairs of words best describes the story?

   A. light-hearted and humorous   C. sad and serious

   B. serious and angry   D. lonely and sad

3. The writer mentioned a superhero named Dee Terrent. Why do you think she has that name?

   A. It is the name that her parents gave her.

   B. She made it up from the word deterrent, meaning able to stop something or someone.

   C. All the good superhero names were already taken.

   D. She thought it would give her superhero powers.

4. The setting of a story is where and when it takes place. In just one or two sentences, describe the setting of this story. Tip: Imagine it as the beginning of a movie. Where is it and when is it happening?

   _____

   _____

Name _____ Date _____

Reading with Expression—Author's Purpose

You probably can't count the number of times you have asked the question "Why?" That is because people naturally want to know the reason for things. Sometimes we are just curious and want information in order to understand something better. (Why are zebras striped?) Sometimes we want to know why in order to make a decision. (Why should I read this book?) Other times we just want to figure out if something is important, necessary, or just for fun. (Why should I save this?)

Everything that you read is written for a purpose. In order to read it with understanding and expression, you need to ask yourself why the author wrote it. Is it to give you information? Is it to persuade or convince you of something? Is it just for fun—to entertain you?

Think about the story you read about superheroes in the Super Powers Police Force. Ask yourself, "Why did the author write this? To inform me? To persuade me? To entertain me?"

- To **inform** you, the author will give you true facts about a subject.
- To **persuade** you, the author will give you reasons for thinking a certain way.
- To **entertain** you, the author will usually present characters with a problem to solve.

So, what was the author's purpose in the story about superheroes? It was to entertain you—just for fun!

Try It!

Now, use what you learned to practice identifying the author's purpose and using it to read with expression. Below are sections of different kinds of writing. First, identify the author's purpose—to **inform**, **persuade**, or **entertain**. Then practice reading each aloud with the right expression.

1. The Texas Longhorn is a symbol of the Old West. It is named for its horns, which can stretch six feet across. These cattle came from those brought by the Spanish to Mexico 500 years ago. _____

2. I think parental controls on TVs are a good thing. Parental controls allow parents to keep their kids from watching, or even accidentally seeing, things they shouldn't. It is especially important for kids who watch TV when their parents aren't home. Don't you agree? _____

3. Things are just not the way they used to be when *I* was a young superhero. These days it seems that *all* kids think that they have remarkable strength or special powers. It is not as if you can just push a button and suddenly become a superhero. Well, most of the time anyway. _____

The next time you read anything, think about why the author might have written it. Knowing the reason for reading will help you read with better understanding and expression!

Lesson 5 *(cont.)*

Name _____ Date _____

Fluency Checkpoint

You have already listened to, practiced, and read the story below. Now it's time to check your reading fluency. Remember, fluency means not just getting the words right, but also reading at a good rate and with expression, or feeling. Reread the story again, as if you were rehearsing it for a performance. Repeat this as many times as necessary so that you can read it fluently.

Tip! Pay special attention to the words in *italics*. When you practice, stress those words—say them a little louder and stronger. After you have practiced with your team, present your final reading to another team. Have that team tell you what you did best and what could use the most improvement. Then switch. You do the same for them as they perform. Finally, complete the evaluation below.

I am a cop on the Super Powers Police Force (SPPF). I have been on the job stopping villains for a long time. Things are just not the way they used to be when *I* was a young superhero. These days it seems that *all* kids think that they have remarkable strength or special powers. It is not as if you can just push a button and suddenly become a superhero. Well, most of the time anyway. There was this relative of mine, who could just push a button on his sleeve and . . . Never mind. That's another story.

As I was saying, today it seems like there are more heroes than there are criminals to catch! The force will accept just about anyone with even the *smallest* super ability. Can they identify if an individual even *has* a superpower anymore? These young "heroes" come in and expect to start immediately. They are so *full* of themselves. They think they can just *skip* the training and go *right* out on the street! Poof! Criminals caught! Just like that! I say, a little spirit and a name such as *"Dee Terrent"* does not a superhero make!

Perhaps you are wondering why I would not be *glad* that there are so many young men and women joining the SPPF. It's pretty simple. Next week will be the date of my 25th anniversary with the force. Although *I* still think I can have an effect on the bad guys who roam the streets, my *boss* feels differently. Tomorrow, I am being moved to a desk job in the police library. What scoundrels am I supposed to catch *there*? *Flies*?

Evaluation

Work in a team of three to get some feedback on your progress with reading fluently. Begin by each taking one of the three paragraphs in the story to practice and get ready to perform.

My team was best at: reading accurately   reading at a good rate   reading with expression

We could really improve on: reading accurately   reading at a good rate   reading with expression

The members of my team were _____, _____, and _____.

The evaluating team included _____, _____, and _____.

© Shell Education

Name _____ Date _____

Phrases

Read these phrases to yourself as you listen to them being read aloud.

toward a <u>balanced</u> future	to go to <u>college</u>	<u>bending</u> my ear
don't <u>forget</u>	the <u>telephone</u> rang	<u>satellites</u> into <u>orbit</u>
down the <u>highway</u>	<u>rhyme</u> or reason	someone with <u>principles</u>
get out and <u>vote</u>	to <u>vote</u>	education and <u>health</u> care

Could you read every word? If not, repeat reading and listening until you can. Then, try reading the phrases on your own without listening.

Story

Read the story to yourself as you listen to it being read aloud. Repeat reading and listening until you know every word.

Just before dinner, **the telephone rang**.

"Will you get that, Randi? I'm up to my neck in dishes," said Mom.

I picked up the phone and said hello politely. The voice on the other end, though, just ignored me and started talking. I didn't want to be rude, so I just listened.

"Who isn't concerned about the future?" he said. Then without stopping, he continued. "What about spending? Is putting **satellites into orbit** more important than **education and health care**? You don't think so, do you?"

I tried to get a word in edgewise, but he just kept going.

"Shouldn't every young person have the chance **to go to college**? And **don't forget** about our older folks."

I couldn't make **rhyme or reason** of what this guy was going on about. Didn't he realize that I was just a kid?

"Wait! I'm just a..." I tried to say, but he wouldn't stop even long enough to let me finish a sentence.

"You need **someone with principles**," he declared. "Someone who will lead this country **down the highway toward a balanced future**. You need Mark Jackson."

"Huh?" I thought. "What is this guy **bending my ear** about?"

"You need Mark Jackson," he repeated. "So, on November 5, **get out and vote**! But, be sure **to vote** for Mark Jackson." Then without even a good-bye, the line went silent.

Mom called from the kitchen. "Who was it, Randi?"

By this time I had realized why the guy on the line didn't let me talk back. It was a recording! I felt kind of silly, so I responded to Mom by saying, "It was just Mark Jackson. He wants you **to vote** for him."

Name _____ Date _____

On Your Own

Sometimes phrases don't really mean what the actual words say. For example, if you read "the time flew by," you know that it doesn't mean a clock with wings flies past! It means the time passed quickly. Look at these phrases. Write what you think they really mean.

1. When I dance, I *have two left feet.* _____

2. I was right and my brother had to *eat his words.* _____

3. When I heard the news, I *hit the ceiling.* _____

4. I can read music, but I also can *play by ear.* _____

5. Let me *give you a hand* with that. _____

Story Questions Main Idea, Cause & Effect, Vocabulary, Critical Thinking

Think about the story you listened to and practiced on page 33. Now, find out how well you understood it! Answer the questions below. You may need to go back and read the story again.

1. Which of these would be the best title for this story?

   A. One-Way Conversation   C. Wait! I'm Just a . . .

   B. Mark Jackson   D. Vote for Me!

2. Randi stayed on the phone to the end. Which reason best tells why Randi didn't hang up?

   A. It is not polite to hang up on someone.

   B. Randi thought the man was talking to him.

   C. Randi wanted to answer the man's questions.

   D. Randi was waiting to see if the man would ask to speak to someone else.

3. What is the meaning of the word *principle* as it is used in the story?

   A. the head of a school

   B. the main or most important

   C. the source of something

   D. moral value

4. At the end of the story, Randi figures out that the phone call was a recording. Which word best describes how Randi felt then: *puzzled, concerned, panicked, embarrassed,* or *angry*? Write your choice and then explain what in the story made you choose it.

   _____

   _____

Name _____ Date _____

Reading with Expression—Figures of Speech

It's hard enough to have to learn and understand the meanings of many words and phrases. But, on top of that, we use many expressions that don't even mean what the words say! For example, if you read in a story that someone is *pulling your leg*, it has nothing to do with a leg or pulling. It really means that someone is kidding or fooling you. If someone *cracks up*, it really means that someone is laughing. These expressions are called **figures of speech**.

Sometimes these figures of speech are funny if you take them to mean exactly what they say. Can you picture someone actually bending your ear or a country being led down the highway? So, in the story when Mom says, *"Will you get that, Randi? I'm up to my neck in dishes,"* she doesn't mean that she is standing in a pile of dishes as high as her neck! What she means, of course, is that she is busy doing the dishes.

Figures of speech are used to make our stories—told or written—more interesting and dramatic. In the story, having Mom say, "I'm up to my neck in dishes," is more interesting than "I'm busy."

When you are reading, it is important to recognize the real meaning of the message—not just the actual words. Then, instead of reading like a robot, you can use your voice to make the story come alive. Of course, a story can't really come alive. That is just a figure of speech!

Try It!

Now, try recognizing and reading figures of speech with expression. First, look at each sentence. The **bold** part is a figure of speech. Write what it really means. Then, practice reading it out loud in a way that shows its meaning.

1. I tried to **get a word in edgewise**, but he just kept going.

   _____

2. I couldn't **make rhyme or reason** of what this guy was going on about.

   _____

3. You need someone who will **lead this country down the highway** toward a balanced future.

   _____

4. What is this guy **bending my ear** about?

   _____

The next time you read this or another story, look for phrases that don't mean what the words actually say. Think about what the phrase really means and then read it with expression that shows its real meaning. Don't read like a robot—make whatever you read come alive!

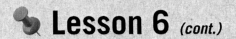

Name _____ Date _____

 # Fluency Checkpoint

You have already listened to, practiced, and read the story below. Now it's time to check your reading fluency. Remember, fluency means not just getting the words right, but also reading at a good rate and with expression, or feeling. Reread the story again, as if you were rehearsing it for a performance. Repeat this as many times as necessary so that you can read it fluently.

Just before dinner, the telephone rang.

"Will you get that, Randi? I'm up to my neck in dishes," said Mom.

I picked up the phone and said hello politely. The voice on the other end, though, just ignored me and started talking. I didn't want to be rude, so I just listened.

"Who isn't concerned about the future?" he said. Then without stopping, he continued. "What about spending? Is putting satellites into orbit more important than education and health care? You don't think so, do you?"

I tried to get a word in edgewise, but he just kept going.

"Shouldn't every young person have the chance to go to college? And don't forget about our older folks."

I couldn't make rhyme or reason of what this guy was going on about. Didn't he realize that I was just a kid?

"Wait! I'm just a . . . " I tried to say, but he wouldn't stop even long enough to let me finish a sentence.

"You need someone with principles," he declared. "Someone who will lead this country down the highway toward a balanced future. You need Mark Jackson."

"Huh?" I thought. "What is this guy bending my ear about?"

"You need Mark Jackson," he repeated. "So, on November 5, get out and vote! But, be sure to vote for Mark Jackson." Then without even a good-bye, the line went silent.

Mom called from the kitchen. "Who was it, Randi?"

By this time I had realized why the guy on the line didn't let me talk back. It was a recording! I felt kind of silly, so I responded to Mom by saying, "It was just Mark Jackson. He wants you to vote for him."

Evaluation

Try something a little different! Read the story again. Pick three different "voices" to use—Mom, Randi, and Mark Jackson. Read the story aloud to someone at home using a different voice for each part.

How did you do? _____

Wasn't it more fun to read this way? _____

Which "part" did you enjoy most? _____

Name _____ Date _____

Phrases

Read these phrases to yourself as you listen to them being read aloud.

blows the <u>roof</u> off	the little <u>pigs</u>	<u>they're</u> not always
a wise <u>observation</u>	<u>vary</u> a little more	<u>basket</u> of goodies
all <u>citizens</u>	as a <u>reader</u>	<u>drawn</u> as big, bad, and scary
to my young <u>daughter</u>	<u>surrounded</u> by images	takes no <u>effort</u>

Could you read every word? If not, repeat reading and listening until you can. Then, try reading the phrases on your own without listening.

An Editorial

An editorial is a special kind of writing that states one person's opinion about a topic. An editorial is intended to be printed in a newspaper or magazine for many people to see.

Read the editorial to yourself as you listen to it being read aloud. Repeat reading and listening until you know every word.

Editorial

As a reader, I enjoy a good story. As a parent, I enjoy sharing stories with my kids. But I have a beef about a few popular children's stories. Specifically, I am referring to ones such as "Little Red Riding Hood" and "The Three Little Pigs." Recently I read these **to my young daughter**. Afterward, she looked puzzled. When I asked what she didn't understand, she said, "I don't understand why the wolf is always the bad guy."

"Wow," I thought. "She didn't just understand; she made **a wise observation**!"

I thought about her comment for a while. In "The Three Little Pigs," the wolf comes by and **blows the roof off** of their house in an effort to get to **the little pigs**. If you think about it, though, the wolf is only doing what wolves do. Like any animal, it looks for food. Face it. Pigs are food for wolves. In fact, pigs are food for many *people*! So, why is the wolf in the story **drawn as big, bad, and scary**?

In "Little Red Riding Hood," another big, bad wolf is in the woods. Wolves live in the woods. What shouldn't be in the woods is a little girl alone with a **basket of goodies**!

My little daughter had a good point. However, I can go one further. In both stories, the big bad wolves get killed in the end. Is this really the kind of message we want to give our young children? I would like to see stories that have wolves as characters who **vary a little more** so that **they're not always** the bad guys. Also, our children are already **surrounded by images** of violence, so why make their stories end with the "bad" character (wolf) being killed?

I ask **all citizens**, especially parents, to stop reading these violent, biased stories to young children. It **takes no effort** to find many other delightful and happy stories to read and share!

—*Janet McDaniel*, Bartlet, NY

Name _____ Date _____

On Your Own

Take a moment to think back about the stories the writer mentions. How are they alike? Different? Write a short paragraph that compares the wolves in each story. If you don't know the stories, write a paragraph that describes what you know and think about wolves.

_____

_____

_____

_____

Editorial Questions Main Idea, Details, Vocabulary, Critical Thinking

Think about the editorial you listened to and practiced on page 37. Now, find out how well you understood it! Answer the questions below. You may need to go back and read the editorial again.

1. Which of these statements best tells the main point the writer is trying to make?
   A. All children's stories are too violent.
   B. Children's stories should not end with a wolf getting killed.
   C. Some children's stories give the wrong messages to kids.
   D. People should not read children's stories to their kids.

2. Based on what the writer said in the editorial, which of the following can you conclude?
   A. The writer is a mother.
   B. The writer is surprised at the little girl's response.
   C. The writer does not think that wolves are necessarily bad.
   D. All of the above.

3. Which of the following words could replace the word *beef* in the editorial?
   A. complaint
   B. meat
   C. strength
   D. cattle

4. In an editorial, the writer is expressing a strong opinion about a topic and is trying to convince the readers to agree. In this editorial, do you think the writer did a good job? Why or why not?

   _____

   _____

   _____

Name _____ Date _____

Reading with Expression— Using Stress to Support a Position

The purpose of an editorial is to get people to think one way or another about something. This is done by triggering certain feelings that may make you change your mind. It is also done by giving examples and reasons why you should agree with a certain opinion. In the editorial you just read, the writer has an opinion. She wants people to stop reading stories like "Little Red Riding Hood" and "The Three Little Pigs" to young children because they show wolves as bad and they are killed at the end. You and other readers may not agree. So, she gives reasons and examples that support her opinion that may get you to agree to her feelings about the topic.

Look at these sentences. Which one of these sentences is more convincing?

Don't read stories to little children that always show a wolf as big, bad, and scary. People sometimes grow up believing that wolves are bad and should be killed on sight.

The first sentence simply asks you to agree with the author. The second sentence is more convincing because it gives you a reason to agree with the author. In an editorial, or in any writing in which the author is trying to persuade someone to feel a certain way, look for how the writer uses examples and reasons to support a position. The author intends these examples to be convincing, so when reading aloud, you will want to stress these points.

Try It!

The word **bias** means an unfair preference for or prejudice against something. The editorial says that some children's stories are biased against wolves. This is the writer's opinion. You may agree or disagree. However, whether or not you agree, think about how the editorial would sound if the author were reading it. She would stress the parts that support her point of view and especially the words that trigger the feelings she wants her readers to have. Take this challenge: Go back to the third paragraph of the editorial. It begins with "I thought about. . . Underline any words or phrases you would stress if reading it aloud. Finally, reread this section without stressing anything. Then read it again, stressing the words and phrases you underlined. Rate how much more convincing it is the second time. Circle your rating:

When you are reading anything that is trying to convince you to act or feel a certain way, keep in mind that these points are stressed to sway your feelings and opinion.

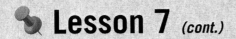

Name _____ Date _____

 # Fluency Checkpoint

You have already listened to, practiced, and read the story below. Now it's time to check your reading fluency. Remember, fluency means not just getting the words right, but also reading at a good rate and with expression, or feeling. Reread the story again, as if you were rehearsing it for a performance. Repeat this as many times as necessary so that you can read it fluently.

> As a reader, I enjoy a good story. As a parent, I enjoy sharing stories with my kids. But I have a beef about a few popular children's stories. Specifically, I am referring to ones such as "Little Red Riding Hood" and "The Three Little Pigs." Recently I read these to my young daughter. Afterward, she looked puzzled. When I asked what she didn't understand, she said, "I don't understand why the wolf is always the bad guy."
>
> "Wow," I thought. "She didn't just understand; she made a wise observation!"
>
> I thought about her comment for a while. In "The Three Little Pigs," the wolf comes by and blows the roof off of their house in an effort to get to the little pigs. If you think about it, though, the wolf is only doing what wolves do. Like any animal, it looks for food. Face it. Pigs are food for wolves. In fact, pigs are food for many *people*! So, why is the wolf in the story drawn as big, bad, and scary?
>
> In "Little Red Riding Hood," another big, bad wolf is in the woods. Wolves live in the woods. What shouldn't be in the woods is a little girl alone with a basket of goodies!
>
> My little daughter had a good point. However, I can go one further. In both stories, the big bad wolves get killed in the end. Is this really the kind of message we want to give our young children? I would like to see stories that have wolves as characters who vary a little more so that they're not always the bad guys. Also, our children are already surrounded by images of violence, so why make their stories end with the "bad" character (wolf) being killed?
>
> I ask all citizens, especially parents, to stop reading these violent, biased stories to young children. It takes no effort to find many other delightful and happy stories to read and share!
>
> —*Janet McDaniel*, Bartlet, NY

Evaluation

Practice reading the editorial one more time. Then, record yourself reading it aloud. Listen to your recording and complete the evaluation below.

My reading was:	smooth	somewhat smooth	choppy
My rate of reading was:	too slow	just right	too fast
My reading expression was:	excellent	good	only fair

I misread and need to practice these words: _____

Name _____ Date _____

Phrases

Read these phrases to yourself as you listen to them being read aloud.

multiple of 3 and 4	a series of numbers	a series of puzzles
ancient Chinese puzzle	my first discovery	about twelve times
my dad's influence	threw in one more thing	showed me a trick
certain characteristics	hidden pictures book	rather play baseball
take a bow	nobody got it	a waste of time
I learned	solve math puzzles	

Could you read every word? If not, repeat reading and listening until you can. Then, try reading the phrases on your own without listening.

Friendly Letter

Read the letter to yourself as you listen to it being read aloud. Repeat reading and listening until you know every word.

April 14, 2007

Dear Kendra,

In your last letter you asked me what was my favorite subject at school. Believe it or not, it's math. I guess it's because of **my dad's influence**. He teaches math in high school. He got me started when I was little. I made **my first discovery** that puzzles are fun with a **hidden pictures book**. Later, I figured out that I especially liked to **solve math puzzles**. Even in the car my dad would give me **a series of numbers** and ask me what comes next. Or, he'd say, "I'm thinking of a number. It's less than 15 but more than 9. It's a **multiple of 3 and 4**." I'd sit there quietly and by the time we got to wherever we were going, I'd have it.

Last week **I learned** about an **ancient Chinese puzzle** based on **certain characteristics**. Actually, it's **a series of puzzles** called Magic Squares. It's easier to just draw you an example than to explain it. So it's at the end of this letter.

Our math teacher challenged us to fill in all the empty blocks with numbers so that if you inserted them across, down, or diagonal you came up with the same sum. Then she **threw in one more thing**. You could only use a number once. At first, **nobody got it**. Todd (that boy that I told you about) claimed it was just **a waste of time**. I think he just didn't want anybody to know he was having trouble. Anyway, after trying and erasing **about twelve times**, I solved it! The teacher had me **take a bow**. Todd made some comment about how I only got it because my dad already **showed me a trick** or something. He was just jealous! I know you would **rather play baseball** than solve math puzzles, but just in case you want to try, I am not going to give you the answer. I'll give you *one* number to get you going, but you have to solve it. When you do, write me back!

Your friend,
Julie

Name _____ Date _____

On Your Own

First, try to solve the Chinese puzzle, using the numbers 1–9. Next, on the lines below, jot down some phrases about what you experienced while trying to solve the puzzle. Next, imagine that you are Julie's friend. In your journal or on a fresh sheet of paper, write a letter back to Julie. Be sure to use correct letter form.

_____

_____

_____

_____

	5	

Letter Questions

Main Idea, Drawing Conclusions, Vocabulary, Critical Thinking

Think about the letter to which you listened and which you practiced on page 41. Now, find out how well you understood it! Answer the questions below. You may need to go back and read the letter again.

1. Which statement best describes the main point Julie tries to make in the letter?
    A. Todd is jealous of her.
    B. Magic Squares are Chinese puzzles.
    C. She learned to love math from her dad.
    D. She enjoys solving puzzles, especially math ones.

2. One of these statements is a fact. The rest are opinions. Which is the fact?
    A. Everyone likes to do puzzles.
    B. Magic Squares is a very old puzzle.
    C. Nobody can solve a Magic Squares puzzle in just one try.
    D. Todd said solving the puzzle was a waste of time because he was having trouble.

3. The word *bow* is said two ways. Which word below rhymes with bow as it is used in the story?
    A. slow   C. owl
    B. cow   D. None of the above.

4. Do you think Kendra shares Julie's love of math? _____
    Why or why not? _____

5. Has Kendra written to Julie before? _____

Name _____ Date _____

 # Reading with Expression—Recognizing Point of View

Imagine that you are standing between a baby and a basketball player. To the baby, you look very big. To the basketball player, you look kind of small. Are you big or small? That depends on **point of view**. Point of view means how something appears (view) from a certain place (point). In the example, even though you are just one size and didn't change, from the baby's point of view, you are big. From the basketball player's point of view, you are small.

Everything you read also has a point of view. The point of view is determined by who is telling the story or giving the information. When you see words such as *I, me, my, us, we,* and *our*, the narrator (storyteller) is writing about his or her own experiences, feelings, and opinions. This is called *first person* point of view. So, if you are the narrator telling about your own experiences, feelings, and opinions, it is called a *personal narrative*.

Other times, you may read something that is written about events, characters, experiences, or information. When you see words such as *he, she, him, her, they, and their,* the narrator is not writing from firsthand knowledge, but rather telling something he or she heard or learned from somewhere else. This is called *third person* point of view. It is as if the storyteller is observing and writing down what he or she sees from a distance.

Try It!

The sentences below are from the letter written by Julie in first person point of view. Rewrite them in third person point of view—as if you were telling the story not as Julie but about Julie.

First Person writing about my own experience, feelings, and opinions *I, me, my, we, us, our*	**Third Person** writing about someone or something learned or heard from somewhere else *he, she, him, her, they, their*

1. I'd sit there quietly and by the time we got to wherever we were going, I'd have it.

   _____

   _____

2. Todd made some comment about how I only got it because my dad already showed me a trick.

   _____

   _____

Name _____ Date _____

 ## Fluency Checkpoint

You have already listened to, practiced, and read the letter below. Now it's time to check your reading fluency. Remember, fluency means not just getting the words right, but also reading at a good rate and with expression, or feeling. Reread the letter again, as if you were rehearsing it for a performance. Repeat this as many times as necessary so that you can read it fluently.

April 14, 2007

Dear Kendra,

In your last letter you asked me what was my favorite subject at school. Believe it or not, it's math. I guess it's because of my dad's influence. He teaches math in high school. He got me started when I was little. I made my first discovery that puzzles are fun with a hidden pictures book. Later, I figured out that I especially liked to solve math puzzles. Even in the car my dad would give me a series of numbers and ask me what comes next. Or, he'd say, "I'm thinking of a number. It's less than 15 but more than 9. It's a multiple of 3 and 4." I'd sit there quietly and by the time we got to wherever we were going, I'd have it.

Last week I learned about an ancient Chinese puzzle based on certain characteristics. Actually, it's a series of puzzles called Magic Squares. It's easier to just draw you an example than to explain it. So it's at the end of this letter.

Our math teacher challenged us to fill in all the empty blocks with numbers so that if you inserted them across, down, or diagonal you came up with the same sum. Then she threw in one more thing. You could only use a number once. At first, nobody got it. Todd (that boy that I told you about) claimed it was just a waste of time. I think he just didn't want anybody to know he was having trouble. Anyway, after trying and erasing about twelve times, I solved it! The teacher had me take a bow. Todd made some comment about how I only got it because my dad already showed me a trick or something. He was just jealous! I know you would rather play baseball than solve math puzzles, but just in case you want to try, I am not going to give you the answer. I'll give you one number to get you going, but you have to solve it. When you do, write me back!

Your friend,
Julie

Evaluation

Evaluate your own reading and understanding of the letter and skills presented in this lesson. Read each statement. Then, circle **true** if it is true in your opinion, and **false** if it is false in your opinion.

1. I know all the words in the letter.   **true   false**

2. I can read the letter fluently—accurately, at a good rate, and with expression.   **true   false**

Name _____ Date _____

Phrases

Read these phrases to yourself as you listen to them being read aloud.

they <u>struggled</u>	<u>cracked</u> the code	believed that <u>Germany</u>
what <u>Germany</u> was planning	<u>invented</u> a code	in <u>theory</u>
nothing <u>prevented</u>	<u>dozens</u> of the best minds	<u>vast</u> numbers
looking for a <u>combination</u>	a <u>rational</u> pattern	
<u>worthy</u> of being called	what was this <u>worth</u>	

Could you read every word? If not, repeat reading and listening until you can. Then, try reading the phrases on your own without listening.

Story

Read the story to yourself as you listen to it being read aloud. Repeat reading and listening until you know every word.

Who is an American hero? There are many well-known names from which to choose. However, there are also **vast numbers** of unknown names that qualify as heroes. Certainly, this includes all soldiers who fought and gave their lives in times of war. Yet, there is one man who helped turn the tide of WWII. He did this not on the battlefield, but from a former school in Arlington, Virginia.

It was the fifth year of the war. **Nothing prevented** the United States from picking up the enemy's messages, but they were in code. **In theory**, any code has **a rational pattern**. It should be just a matter of figuring it out. **Dozens of the best minds** at the time were put to the task of breaking the code. Yet, **they struggled**. Some **believed that Germany** had finally **invented a code** that couldn't be broken.

Not David Mead. In 1942, he was studying English at college. He loved doing crossword puzzles. That summer, Mead left college to join the army. He wanted to help in the war effort.

Between his regular army duties, Mead set his mind on the code. Using his skill at crossword puzzles, he spent months staring at the numbers that came in over the wire. He was **looking for a combination** that would give the key. He got a break when a Japanese operator sent almost identical messages by mistake. That did it! David Mead **cracked the code**.

What was this worth? The United States then knew and could react to **what Germany was planning**. Cracking the code played one of the most important parts in winning WWII. This makes David Mead **worthy of being called** an "American hero."

Lesson 9 (cont.)

Name _____ Date _____

On Your Own

Did you catch the meanings of these phrases in the story? Go back and find each one. Then, write a different sentence of your own using the phrase.

1. turn the tide: _____

   _____

2. in theory: _____

   _____

3. vast numbers: _____

   _____

4. got a break: _____

   _____

Story Questions Main Idea, Details, Vocabulary, Critical Thinking

Think about the story you listened to and practiced on page 45. Now, find out how well you understood it! Answer the questions below. You may need to go back and read the story again.

1. Which of these would be the best title for this story?
   A. World War II
   B. A Secret Code
   C. An American Hero
   D. In the Army

2. Number these statements 1–4 to show the order that the events happened.
   _____ Mead spent months trying to break the code.
   _____ Mead left school to join the army.
   _____ Mead cracked the secret code.
   _____ World War II began.

3. Which of the following word pairs are not synonyms—words that mean almost the same thing?
   A. rational—sensible   C. react—respond
   B. worthy—deserving   D. prevented—permitted

4. The story doesn't say so directly, but you can tell two of the countries that were enemies of the United States in WWII? Name them below.

   _____ and _____

#50279—Increasing Fluency with High Frequency Word Phrases   © *Shell Education*

Name _____ Date _____

 # Reading with Expression—Chunk for Smoothness

Does your reading ever sound choppy? If so, you might be reading one word at a time. Below is a long sentence from the story you read. Try reading it just one word at a time:

Using / his / skill / at / crossword / puzzles / he / spent / months / staring / at / the / numbers / that / came / in / over / the / wire.

As you read, your eyes focused on each word separately. But, you can train your eyes to look at groups of words at the same time. Try it now.

Using his skill / at crossword puzzles / he spent months / staring at the numbers / that came in / over the wire.

This time your eyes grouped related words together. The sentence had only *six* parts instead of *nineteen* individual words. As you read in chunks, it sounded better, but is still a little choppy. There are still too many breaks. So, how do you smooth out the choppiness even more? Suppose that you grouped these words *in your head* <u>before</u> you actually read them. Your brain would recognize the meaning of the chunks instead of just individual words and tell you in an instant how to combine chunks so that they make the most sense when read aloud. Try reading the sentence now:

Using his skill at crossword puzzles / he spent months staring at the numbers / that came in over the wire.

That sounds nice and smooth and is easier to understand, too. The trick is to look at the words ahead of where you are. Let your eyes recognize the words and your amazing brain group them into chunks that have meaning. So when do you have time to do this while you are reading more than one sentence? In that instant when you stop between sentences at the final period, question mark, or exclamation point! Sometimes, you get even get a quick peek ahead when you pause at a comma!

Try It!

Now, use what you learned about reading in chunks for smoothness. On a piece of paper, write the second paragraph from the story on page 45. Can you use your amazing brain to figure out how it should be read so that it is smooth and easy to understand? Draw in lines (/) to separate the sentences and parts of sentences into chunks for smooth reading! **Note:** Some short sentences should be read in a single chunk. Medium length sentences often have only two chunks, but sometimes have more.

 The next time you read this or another story, remember what you have learned about chunking. First, glance over it to note where there are built-in signals (periods, question marks, and commas). Then, before you read each sentence completely, have your eyes look quickly at all the words in the sentence and let your mind group them in chunks.

Lesson 9 (cont.)

Name _____ Date _____

Fluency Checkpoint

You have already listened to, practiced, and read the story below. Now it's time to check your reading fluency. Remember, fluency means not just getting the words right, but also reading at a good rate and with expression, or feeling. Reread the story again, as if you were rehearsing it for a performance. Repeat this as many times as necessary so that you can read it fluently.

Who is an American hero? There are many well-known names to choose from. However, there are also vast numbers of unknown names that qualify as heroes. Certainly this includes all soldiers who fought and gave their lives in times of war. Yet, there is one man who helped turn the tide of WWII. He did this not on the battlefield, but from a former school in Arlington, Virginia.

It was the fifth year of the war. Nothing prevented the United States from picking up the enemy's messages, but they were in code. In theory, any code has a rational pattern. It should be just a matter of figuring it out. Dozens of the best minds at the time were put to the task of breaking the code. Yet, they struggled. Some believed that Germany had finally invented a code that couldn't be broken.

Not David Mead. In 1942, he was studying English at college. He loved doing crossword puzzles. That summer, Mead left college to join the army. He wanted to help in the war effort.

Between his regular army duties, Mead set his mind on the code. Using his skill at crossword puzzles, he spent months staring at the numbers that came in over the wire. He was looking for a combination that would give the key. He got a break when a Japanese operator sent almost identical messages by mistake. That did it! David Mead cracked the code.

What was this worth? The United States then knew and could react to what Germany was planning. Cracking the code played one of the most important parts in winning WWII. This makes David Mead worthy of being called an American hero.

Evaluation

How *smooth* are you? Can you tell when a sentence is chunked so that it reads smoothly? Read each sentence both ways. Then circle **A** or **B** as your pick for the smoothest way to read it.

1. A. Yet / there is one man / who helped turn the tide / of WWII.

   B. Yet there / is one / man who helped turn / the tide of WWII.

2. A. The United / States then knew and / could react to what / Germany was planning.

   B. The United States then knew / and could react to / what Germany was planning.

#50279—Increasing Fluency with High Frequency Word Phrases
© Shell Education

Name _____ Date _____

Phrases

Read these phrases to yourself as you listen to them being read aloud.

cleared <u>bushes</u>	planted little <u>flags</u>	<u>official</u> <u>dinosaur</u> hunter
no living <u>dinosaurs</u>	a whole <u>dinosaur</u> skeleton	for <u>instance</u>
<u>limited</u> number	not the <u>volume</u>	<u>expanded</u> my thinking
trapped in <u>mud</u>	go one <u>further</u>	climbed <u>slopes</u>
around <u>dig</u> areas	<u>dig</u> for dinosaurs	<u>dig</u> for an explanation

Could you read every word? If not, repeat reading and listening until you can. Then, try reading the phrases on your own without listening.

Story

Read the story to yourself as you listen to it being read aloud. Repeat reading and listening until you know every word.

Like most kids, dinosaurs always interested me. When I was little, I wanted to grow up to be an **official dinosaur hunter**. I knew that there were **no living dinosaurs**. I wanted to dig for their bones. I was going to find **a whole dinosaur skeleton**. It would be one that no one had ever seen before. I'd be famous! They would name it after me—*Bryanosaurus*!

Now, I have **expanded my thinking**. No doubt dinosaurs existed. Plenty of people have **cleared bushes, climbed slopes**, and **planted little flags around dig areas**. For some reason, they know where to look. It's usually because someone has found a fossil or a bone sticking right out of the ground. This bothers me. They say that dinosaur bones are millions of years old. **Trapped in mud**, layer upon layer of soil covered them. Why, then, are so many bones found at or near the surface? If any, a very **limited number** of dinosaur bones should be at the top, but certainly **not the volume** of bones that have been found by people practically tripping over them.

I'll **go one further**. If dinosaurs were buried so long ago, where are all the bones of the animals that lived between then and now? **For instance**, a farmer finds a bone in his field. Where are the bones of the countless animals, and for that matter the people, who lived and died there after the dinosaurs?

Perhaps I still will grow up to be a dinosaur hunter—not to **dig for dinosaurs**, but to **dig for an explanation** to my questions about them.

Name _____ Date _____

On Your Own

How did the author's view of dinosaurs change over time? Write three or four sentences to make "then and now" comparisons.

_____

_____

_____

_____

_____

Story Questions Main Idea, Recognizing Tense, Vocabulary, Critical Thinking

Think about the story you listened to and practiced on page 49. Now find out how well you understood it! Answer the questions below. You may need to go back and read the story again.

1. Which best tells what the whole story is about, or its main idea?
    A. The author wants to be a dinosaur hunter.
    B. The author wants to understand why people dig for dinosaur bones.
    C. The author does not believe that dinosaurs really existed.
    D. The author has unanswered questions about finding dinosaur bones.

2. Which of the following things can you tell about the author from reading the story?
    A. The author is a girl.
    B. The author's name is Bryan.
    C. The author wants to be famous.
    D. None of the above.

3. In which sentence is the word *dig* used as an adjective (describing word)?
    A. They planted little flags around the dig area.
    B. I wanted to dig for dinosaurs.
    C. The dig was surrounded by bushes.
    D. I had to dig for an explanation.

4. The author is bothered by two things. They are stated as questions in the story. What are they? Find these questions and complete them below.

    Why _____ ?

    If _____ ?

5. After reading the story, do the questions the author raises bother you, too? Why or why not? _____

    _____

Name _____ Date _____

📖 Reading with Expression—Tuning In to Final Punctuation

You know that the period, question mark, or exclamation point at the end of a sentence marks the end of a thought and signals you to stop. But, that final punctuation mark does much more. It tells you how to use your voice to read the sentence. Watch what your voice does as you read these sentences:

You know it.   You know it?   You know it!

Notice how your voice goes down and trails off when the sentence ends with a period. At the end of a question, you voice rises up. In an exclamation, your voice is higher and ends sharply. Now try these:

I'd be famous.   I'd be famous?   I'd be famous!

Look at these sentences from the story. First, read them like a robot—without changing your voice at the end. Then, read them using the final punctuation as your guide to reading them with expression.

> Perhaps I will still grow up to be a dinosaur hunter
> Why, then, are so many bones found at or near the surface
> I'd be famous They would name it after me—*Bryanosaurus*

> Perhaps I will still grow up to be a dinosaur hunter**.**
> Why, then, are so many bones found at or near the surface**?**
> I'd be famous**!** They would name it after me—*Bryanosaurus***!**

When you are reading, don't just stop at the final punctuation of a sentence. Use it as a signal that tells you how to read the sentence with expression. Remember, a sentence ending with a period signals that your voice drops down a little at the end. A question mark tells you to make your voice higher at the end. An exclamation point signals excitement or surprise, so your voice goes higher and ends sharply.

Try It!

Now, use what you learned about final punctuation as a signal for how to read a sentence. First, insert a period (.), question mark (?), or exclamation point (!) to each sentence. Then, write what your voice should be doing at the end—*dropping a little, going up,* or *rising and ending sharply.*

1. Why are there so many bones on or near the surface ( ) _____

2. Wow ( ) I'd never thought of that ( ) _____

3. How is it that dinosaur bones are found so easily ( ) _____

Name _____ Date _____

 Fluency Checkpoint

You have already listened to, practiced, and read the story below. Now it's time to check your reading fluency. Remember, fluency means not just getting the words right, but also reading at a good rate and with expression, or feeling. Reread the story again, as if you were rehearsing it for a performance. Repeat this as many times as necessary so that you can read it fluently.

> Like most kids, dinosaurs always interested me. When I was little, I wanted to grow up to be an official dinosaur hunter. I knew that there were no living dinosaurs. I wanted to dig for their bones. I was going to find a whole dinosaur skeleton. It would be one that no one had ever seen before. I'd be famous! They would name it after me— *Bryanosaurus*!
>
> Now, I have expanded my thinking. No doubt dinosaurs existed. Plenty of people have cleared bushes, climbed slopes, and planted little flags around dig areas. For some reason, they know where to look. It's usually because someone has found a fossil or a bone sticking right out of the ground. This bothers me. They say that dinosaur bones are millions of years old. Trapped in mud, layer upon layer of soil covered them. Why, then, are so many bones found at or near the surface? If any, a very limited number of dinosaur bones should be at the top, but certainly not the volume of bones that have been found by people practically tripping over them.
>
> I'll go one further. If dinosaurs were buried so long ago, where are all the bones of the animals that lived between then and now? For instance, a farmer finds a bone in his field. Where are the bones of the countless animals, and for that matter the people, who lived and died there after the dinosaurs?
>
> Perhaps I still will grow up to be a dinosaur hunter—not to dig for dinosaurs, but to dig for an explanation to my questions about them.

Evaluation

Work with a partner to evaluate your fluency progress. Each of you read the story above three times out loud. Have your partner complete the chart below about your reading.

Compared to first reading . . .	Second Reading (yes/no)	Third Reading (yes/no)
Accuracy improved?		
Rate of reading improved?		
Reading with expression improved?		

Name _____ Date _____

Phrases

Read these phrases to yourself as you listen to them being read aloud.

in a tall <u>tower</u>	<u>slide</u> that dish	<u>baked</u> him a special <u>supper</u>
the <u>prince</u> was <u>frightened</u>	had <u>zero</u> luck	feeling <u>terrible</u>
<u>bees'</u> honey and <u>cream</u>	<u>beneath</u> the <u>tower</u>	made the <u>dangerous</u> climb
just <u>hung</u> around	his hopes <u>failed</u> him	his <u>favorite</u> dessert
<u>plenty</u> of princesses	<u>wore</u> the right shoe size	three handsome <u>princes</u>

Could you read every word? If not, repeat reading and listening until you can. Then, try reading the phrases on your own without listening.

Story

Read the story to yourself as you listen to it being read aloud. Repeat reading and listening until you know every word.

There were once **three handsome princes**. The youngest was unhappy. It seems that his two older brothers had married and lived happily ever after. The oldest found his princess at a ball. She just **wore the right shoe size**. The middle brother spotted one **in a tall tower**. He **made the dangerous climb** from **beneath the tower** to the top by way of her really long hair. There were **plenty of princesses** in the area, but the youngest prince **had zero luck** with the ladies. So he **just hung around** the castle **feeling terrible**.

One evening, his mom (the Queen) **baked him a special supper**. He just picked at it. Then, she presented **his favorite dessert**—cake with **bees' honey and cream**. Still hoping to cheer him up, she said, "Why don't you walk down to the garden and have your dessert by the well?"

"Ok, I guess," he answered without a hint of excitement. He walked down the path. He sat on the bench next to the well.

"What's wrong with you?" asked a voice. At first **the prince was frightened**. "Over here," said the voice sweetly.

The prince looked toward the well hoping to see a lovely princess attached to the voice. But, **his hopes failed him**. Instead, there was a frog. "Oh," he muttered, disappointed. "I so wanted you to be a princess."

"Really?" she said. "Haven't you heard the tales about us frogs? Sometimes if you are nice to a frog, it turns into a prince—or a princess, in this case."

Suddenly, he perked up. "Are you a princess?" he asked.

"In a manner of speaking," she replied. "How about you **slide that dish** of cream and honey cake my way?"

The prince did so. When the frog had finished the dessert and was cleaning her face with her tongue, the prince spoke. "You said you were a princess. I've been nice to you. Now show me what kind of princess you are."

"You're lookin' at her, sweetie. I'm a *frog* princess. But, thanks for the dessert!" And with that she hopped back into the well.

Lesson 11 (cont.)

Name _____ Date _____

On Your Own

Did you catch the meanings of these phrases in the story? Go back and find each one. Then, write what it means in your own words.

1. He just hung around: _____

_____

2. His hopes failed him: _____

_____

3. He perked up: _____

_____

4. You're lookin' at her: _____

_____

Story Questions Main Idea, Making Inferences, Vocabulary, Critical Thinking

Think about the story you listened to and practiced on page 53. Now, find out how well you understood it! Answer the questions below. You may need to go back and read the story again.

1. Which of these would be the best title for this story?
   A. The Frog Prince   C. The Frog Princess
   B. Zero Luck   D. Down at the Well

2. Which of these statements is false?
   A. The youngest prince is handsome.
   B. The queen tries to cheer up her youngest son.
   C. The frog tricks the prince into giving her his dessert.
   D. The frog is a beautiful princess in disguise.

3. What is the meaning of the word *well* as it is used in the story?
   A. in a good or skilled way
   B. healthy, in good health
   C. fully and thoroughly
   D. a hole in the ground for getting water

4. The story doesn't say so directly, but it refers to princesses in two other fairy tales. Which two?
   A. Cinderella and Snow White
   B. Snow White and the Seven Dwarfs
   C. Cinderella and Rapunzel
   D. Rapunzel and Goldilocks

Name _____ Date _____

Reading with Expression—Preparing for Surprises

When you want to surprise people, you don't tell them what is going to happen. A surprise only works when it is not expected. You lead someone to expect one thing and then you do something else that is completely unexpected. Surprise!

This story had two surprises! The first one was a twist—something opposite of what you expect. You probably already know that in most fairy tales it is the princess who is hoping to meet a handsome prince. Here, it is the handsome prince that hopes to find a princess. When you first listened to this story read aloud, did you figure out the twist?

The second surprise comes at the end. A fairy tale usually has a predictable ending—everything turns out well and the characters live happily ever after. When the frog tells the prince, "Haven't you heard the tales about us frogs? Sometimes if you are nice to a frog, it turns into a prince—or a princess, in this case," you expect that she will turn into a princess in the end. Surprise! She doesn't!

So, how do you as a reader prepare your listeners for a surprise? The trick is to read the parts leading up to a surprise in a way that goes along with what the listeners expect. Then, change your voice to stress the surprise part. For example, in the story, you would read the prince's statement, "You said you were a princess. I've been nice to you. Now show me what kind of princess you are," without stressing anything. The listeners will be thinking that the frog is about to return the prince's kindness by turning into a beautiful princess. Then, when you read, "You're lookin' at her, sweetie. I'm a *frog* princess," stress the word *lookin'* a little bit, and the word *frog* even more.

Practice reading this story again. Experiment with changing your voice to prepare listeners for the surprise.

Try It!

In addition to the surprises above, this fairy tale also uses humor to create unexpected surprises. Did you recognize the parts that were meant to be unexpected and funny? Finish each statement below.

1. Instead of saying the oldest prince married Cinderella, the story said _____

    _____

2. Instead of saying the middle prince married Rapunzel, the story said _____

    _____

3. Instead of asking for the dessert, the frog said _____

    _____

The next time you read this or another story that contains surprises, pay special attention to how the author "sets up" the reader for a twist or a surprise ending. Then, practice reading it out loud to get the best effect.

Name _____ Date _____

Fluency Checkpoint

You have already listened to, practiced, and read the story below. Now it's time to check your reading fluency. Reread the story again, as if you were rehearsing it for a performance.

There were once three handsome princes. The youngest was unhappy. It seems that his two older brothers had married and lived happily ever after. The oldest found his princess at a ball. She just wore the right shoe size. The middle brother spotted one in a tall tower. He made the dangerous climb from beneath the tower to the top by way of her really long hair. There were plenty of princesses in the area, but the youngest prince had zero luck with the ladies. So he just hung around the castle feeling terrible.

One evening, his mom (the Queen) baked him a special supper. He just picked at it. Then, she presented his favorite dessert—cake with bees' honey and cream. Still hoping to cheer him up, she said, "Why don't you walk down to the garden and have your dessert by the well?"

"Ok, I guess," he answered without a hint of excitement. He walked down the path. He sat on the bench next to the well.

"What's wrong with you?" asked a voice. At first the prince was frightened. "Over here," said the voice sweetly.

The prince looked toward the well hoping to see a lovely princess attached to the voice. But, his hopes failed him. Instead, there was a frog. "Oh," he muttered, disappointed. "I so wanted you to be a princess."

"Really?" she said. "Haven't you heard the tales about us frogs? Sometimes if you are nice to a frog, it turns into a prince—or a princess, in this case."

Suddenly he perked up. "Are you a princess?" he asked.

"In a manner of speaking," she replied. "How about you slide that dish of cream and honey cake my way?"

The prince did so. When the frog had finished the dessert and was cleaning her face with her tongue, the prince spoke. "You said you were a princess. I've been nice to you. Now show me what kind of princess you are."

"You're lookin' at her, sweetie. I'm a *frog* princess. But, thanks for the dessert!" And with that she hopped back into the well.

Evaluation

Evaluate how fluently you can read this story. First, read it aloud to someone at home who is older than you are, such as a parent. Then, explain that you are practicing reading fluently—that is, accurately, at a good speed, and with expression. Ask your listener if he or she "got it" (the surprises and the humor) and if you read it in a way that was understandable and enjoyable.

Name _____ Date _____

Phrases

Read these phrases to yourself as you listen to them being read aloud.

spin a tale	in advance	across the globe
fancy myself a poet	clearly labeled	India seemed much farther
hurried to the bay	everywhere around us	of a journey
the route to go	a local sloop called *Sue*	lungs filled up
the crew	heard the whistle	I yelled
fastened up our sails	our push-off was successful	A poet

Could you read every word? If not, repeat reading and listening until you can. Then, try reading the phrases on your own without listening.

Poem

Read the poem to yourself as you listen to it being read aloud. Repeat reading and listening until you know every word.

I **fancy myself a poet**.
Allow me to **spin a tale**,
Of a journey across the globe,
And how I did set sail.

I thought that I'd be captain
And just my dog **the crew**.
The two of us were going
On **a local sloop called** *Sue*.

I planned the trip **in advance**,
I knew **the route to go**.
My map was **clearly labeled**
With how the wind would blow.

When I **heard the whistle**,
We **hurried to the bay**.
I **fastened up our sails**,
And we were on our way!

Our push-off was successful.
We'd sailed away at last.
The land was way behind us,
When suddenly I gasped!

Everywhere around us,
Nothing could be seen,
Except for endless water,
And not a stick of green.

It was then I panicked.
My **lungs filled up** with air.
I yelled, "What was I thinking?
What am I doing here?"

As fast as I could manage,
I turned the sloop around.
Sailing seemed to sound like fun,
Until there was no ground!

Just twenty minutes later,
I stepped back on the shore.
India seemed much farther
Than it had before.

So now I am **a poet**.
And if again I try
To see the world around me,
I am going to fly!

Lesson 12 *(cont.)*

Name _____ Date _____

On Your Own

<u>Will</u> you <u>read</u> a <u>poem</u>? <u>It</u> won't <u>take</u> you <u>long</u>. Just <u>listen</u> <u>for</u> the <u>rhythm</u> It's <u>something</u> <u>like</u> a <u>song</u>.

In this one there are three beats To follow on each line. Now notice there's a pattern Of the lines that rhyme.

There are many kinds of poems. Some rhyme and some don't. Some have a pattern of beats called rhythm. In the poem above, there is a pattern of three matching stressed beats in each line. In the first part, the stressed beats are underlined. Try to clap the rhythm as you read the words out loud. Now, read the second part. Underline the stressed beats. Finally, answer the questions below.

1. What is the rhyming pattern of this poem? _____

   _____

2. Is it the same or different from the poem on page 57? _____

   _____

Poem Questions

Main Idea, Making Generalizations, Vocabulary, Critical Thinking

Think about the poem you listened to and practiced on page 57. Now find out how well you understood it! Answer the questions below. You may need to go back and read the poem again.

1. Which best tells what the poem is about, or its main idea?
   A. Everyone wants to go on an adventure to see the world.
   B. Sailing out to sea alone is a foolish idea.
   C. A dog does not make a good crew.
   D. Flying is safer than sailing.

2. Which of the following lines are clues that the poem is made up, not true?
   A. *Allow me to spin a tale*, because *spin* means *invent*.
   B. *Just twenty minutes later*, because they couldn't have gone far enough to see no land.
   C. Both A and B.
   D. Neither A nor B, because the poem is about a true experience.

3. The poem uses the word *sloop* twice without telling you what it means. Based on the words and what the poem is about, what do you think *sloop* means?

   _____

   _____

© Shell Education

Name _____ Date _____

 # Reading with Expression—Getting the Rhythm

When reading a story aloud, you use your voice to read with expression. You make your voice go higher or lower on certain words. You sometimes raise or lower the loudness. You do these things to read poetry with expression, too!

Poems generally have something, though, that stories don't—rhythm. Rhythm is a regular pattern of beats that makes some poems sound musical. You use your voice to create the rhythm of stressed and unstressed beats. The poem you read about sailing away is one of these types of poems. Can you recognize the rhythm? Look at the first lines of the poem at the right. The stressed beats appear in **bold** and have a little accent mark (ˊ) above them. Try reading the lines in rhythm.

> I **fán**cy my**sélf** a **pó**et.
> Al**lów** me to **spín** a **tále**,
> Of a **jóurn**ey ac**róss** the **glóbe**,
> And **hów** I **díd** set **sáil**.

Notice that sometimes only part of a word gets the stressed beat. Also, notice that, sometimes, to keep the rhythm regular, you need to tie some syllables together, such as *Of a* in line 3. Practice the rhythm by whisper-reading it to yourself two more times. Then, join your classmates in choral reading the poem. Repeat until everyone in the group is reading in perfect rhythm!

Try It!

You have practiced reading the first part of the poem in rhythm. Now, use what you have learned. First, get the beat of the lines. The stressed beats are marked in each first line to get you started. Next, you mark the rest of the stressed beats. Practice reading these until you have the rhythm correct. Then, practice reading the whole poem in rhythm. Finally, when you are ready, read the entire poem in rhythm to a partner or to someone at home.

> I thoúght that Í'd be cáptain,
> And just my dog the crew.
> The two of us were going
> On a local sloop called *Sue*.
>
> I plánned the tríp in advánce,
> I knew the route to go.
> My map was clearly labeled
> With how the wind would blow.

> Whén I héard the whístle,
> We hurried to the bay.
> I fastened up our sails,
> And we were on our way!
>
> Our púsh-off wás succéssful.
> We'd sailed away at last.
> The land was way behind us,
> When suddenly I gasped!

 The next time you read this or another poem, look for a pattern of beats that creates the rhythm. This will help you read the poem with expression!

Name _____ Date _____

 Fluency Checkpoint

You have already listened to, practiced, and read the poem below. Now, it's time to check your reading fluency. Remember, fluency means not just getting the words right, but also reading at a good rate and with expression, or feeling. Reread the poem again, as if you were rehearsing it for a performance. Repeat this as many times as necessary so that you can read it fluently.

I fancy myself a poet.
Allow me to spin a tale,
Of a journey across the globe,
And how I did set sail.

I thought that I'd be captain
And just my dog the crew.
The two of us were going
On a local sloop called Sue.

I planned the trip in advance,
I knew the route to go.
My map was clearly labeled
With how the wind would blow.

When I heard the whistle,
We hurried to the bay.
I fastened up our sails,
And we were on our way!

Our push-off was successful.
We'd sailed away at last.
The land was way behind us,
When suddenly I gasped!

Everywhere around us,
Nothing could be seen,
Except for endless water,
And not a stick of green.

It was then I panicked.
My lungs filled up with air.
I yelled, "What was I thinking?
What am I doing here?"

As fast as I could manage,
I turned the sloop around.
Sailing seemed to sound like fun,
Until there was no ground!

Just twenty minutes later,
I stepped back on the shore.
India seemed much farther
Than it had before.

So now I am a poet.
And if again I try
To see the world around me,
I am going to fly!

Evaluation

Think back over this whole lesson. By the end, you will have formed some opinions. Answer each question with your opinion. Remember, an opinion is what you think. It is neither right nor wrong.

1. Which is easier for you—reading poetry or reading stories?

   _____

2. Do you think the poem is more like a story or more like a song?

   _____

3. How many times do you think you need to practice to read a poem in perfect rhythm?

   _____

Name _____ Date _____

Phrases

Read these phrases to yourself as you listen to them being read aloud.

to take <u>kids</u>	<u>visitors</u> are <u>treated</u>	<u>glance</u> inside the <u>tents</u>
soldiers eating <u>beans</u>	<u>societies</u> of long ago	<u>eager</u> to learn
outdoor <u>fort</u>	<u>claim</u> that <u>frequently</u>	<u>kids</u> don't take
<u>treated</u> for a <u>wound</u>	<u>asleep</u> on a cot	a <u>blend</u> of <u>adventure</u> and history
<u>lacks</u> <u>magic</u>	<u>Native</u> American life	water <u>boiling</u>
<u>social</u> <u>habits</u>	<u>bark</u> on the trees	<u>extra</u> special
alive and <u>personal</u>		

Could you read every word? If not, repeat reading and listening until you can. Then, try reading the phrases on your own without listening.

A Review

Read this review of a field trip to yourself as you listen to it being read aloud. Repeat reading and listening until you know every word.

> Last week, our fourth grade class visited the Museum of Natural History. It was not what I had expected. I thought I would see dull exhibits. Instead, it was something **extra special**.
>
> This is a great place **to take kids** that is both fun and educational. Here, **visitors are treated** with **a blend of adventure and history**. Instead of just imagining, they can actually view the **societies of long ago**.
>
> One of the best displays is the **outdoor fort**. There are some **soldiers eating beans** out of a tin can. **Glance inside the tents**. In one, there is a man on a cot. He is being **treated for a wound** on his head. Another is **asleep on a cot** beside him. The scene is so real that you almost feel as if you are there.
>
> Inside, there are recreations of **Native American life**. Here you can witness the **social habits** of different tribes. Again, this is done so realistically! There is real **bark on the trees**. There is even **water boiling** in a pot over a fire.
>
> Parents and teachers **claim that frequently kids don't take** an interest in history. Maybe this is because it seems so unreal to us. Just reading about it **lacks magic**. At the museum, though, it seems more **alive and personal**. After visiting, I can see better how the lives of those in the past are reflected in our lives today. It actually made me **eager to learn** more!
>
> In conclusion, to take a trip back in time, the Natural History Museum is the place to go!

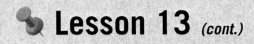

Name _____ Date _____

On Your Own

Complete each sentence with a phrase from the story.

1. The Museum of American History is a great place _____
2. Visitors are treated with _____
3. Inside, there are recreations of _____
4. At the museum, history seems more _____
5. Instead of imagining, you can view the_____

Review Questions

Main Idea, Drawing Conclusions, Vocabulary, Critical Thinking

Think about the review you listened to and practiced on page 61. You have read the review. Now, find out how well you understood it! Answer the questions below. You may need to go back and read the review again.

1. Which best tells what the whole review is about, or its main idea?
   A. The writer thinks that the museum is a great place go.
   B. The outdoor fort at the museum is very realistic.
   C. Frequently, kids don't take much interest in history.
   D. The museum is a place to learn about Native American life.

2. Which of the following would you least likely see at the American History Museum?
   A. A real soldier's uniform from the Civil War.
   B. A canoe made from animal skins.
   C. A model of an Egyptian pyramid.
   D. A display of tools used to grind corn and make clay pottery.

3. The word *treated* is used twice in the review. Which two meanings does it have?
   A. to pay for someone else *and* to apply a coating
   B. to apply a coating *and* to provide something enjoyable
   C. to try to heal or cure *and* to pay for someone else
   D. to provide something enjoyable *and* to try to heal or cure

4. The writer enjoyed the museum and recommended it as a good place to take kids. In this review, did the writer convince you that going to this museum would be fun for kids? Give your answer and then explain why or why not.

   _____

   _____

   _____

   _____

#50279—*Increasing Fluency with High Frequency Word Phrases*   © *Shell Education*

Name _____ Date _____

Reading with Expression—Pronunciation for Accuracy

Sometimes when you are reading you will come across a word you don't know how to say. This may be an English word or, sometimes, a word in another language. For English words, you can look up the pronunciation in a dictionary. For new terms and unfamiliar words in other languages, oftentimes the writer provides the pronunciation. However, to say the words correctly, you need to be able to use a **pronunciation key**. This is the set of symbols that show you how to pronounce sounds.

Take a look at these sounds:

ă	p**a**t	ĕ	p**e**t	ŏ	p**o**t	o͞o	t**oo**th	ŭ	c**u**t
ā	p**ay**	ē	b**ee**	ō	t**oe**	o͝o	f**oo**t	ûr	t**er**m, w**or**d
âr	c**are**	ĭ	p**i**t	ô	f**or**, h**orr**id			ə	**a**bout, circ**u**s
ä	f**a**ther	ī	p**ie**, b**y**	oi	n**oi**se			ər	butt**er**
		îr	p**ier**	ou	**ou**t			zh	vi**s**ion

Here are four English words you probably don't know how to say. Practice using the key to pronounce them correctly.

echidna (ēkĭd nə)   ***pneumatic*** (no͞o măt ĭk)   ***tenacious*** (tĭ nā shəs)
sapphire (săf īr)

Often, names of people, places, and things are unfamiliar. Now use the key to help you pronounce these names.

Miguel (mē gĕl)   ***Mr. Piquet*** (pĭ kā)   ***The Wampanoag*** (wäm pə nō ag) ***Indians***

Carpathian (kär pā thē ən) ***Mountains***   ***Treaty of Versailles*** (vər sī)
Peace Corps (kôr)

Try It!

Now, use what you have learned to take the "Pronunciation Challenge." Use the guide to read each pronunciation. Then, find the actual word in the review. Write it (spelled correctly) on the line.

1. (myoo sē əm) _____
2. (sēn) _____
3. (sə sī ə tēz) _____
4. (sōl jərz) _____

5. (frē kwənt lē) _____
6. (ē gər) _____
7. (rē flĕkt ĭd) _____
8. (kən klo͞o zhən)_____

The next time you come across a word you don't know how to pronounce, first see if the writer gives you a pronunciation, then look in the dictionary for the pronunciation key. Use it to help you figure out correct sounds in the word and how to say them.

Name _____ Date _____

Fluency Checkpoint

You have already listened to, practiced, and read the review below. Now it's time to check your reading fluency. Remember, fluency means not just getting the words right, but also reading at a good rate and with expression, or feeling. Reread the review again, as if you were rehearsing it for a performance. Repeat this as many times as necessary so that you can read it fluently.

> Last week, our fourth grade class visited the Museum of Natural History. It was not what I had expected. I thought I would see dull exhibits. Instead, it was something extra special.
>
> This is a great place to take kids that is both fun and educational. Here, visitors are treated with a blend of adventure and history. Instead of just imagining, they can actually view the societies of long ago.
>
> One of the best displays is the outdoor fort. There are some soldiers eating beans out of a tin can. Glance inside the tents. In one, there is a man on a cot. He is being treated for a wound on his head. Another is asleep on a cot beside him. The scene is so real that you almost feel as if you are there.
>
> Inside, there are recreations of Native American life. Here you can witness the social habits of different tribes. Again, this is done so realistically! There is real bark on the trees. There is even water boiling in a pot over a fire.
>
> Parents and teachers claim that frequently kids don't take an interest in history. Maybe this is because it seems so unreal to us. Just reading about it lacks magic. At the museum, though, it seems more alive and personal. After visiting, I can see better how the lives of those in the past are reflected in our lives today. It actually made me eager to learn more!
>
> In conclusion, to take a trip back in time, the Natural History Museum is the place to go!

Evaluation

Focus for a moment on accuracy—getting the words right. Think back to your reading of the review before and after the lesson on using a pronunciation key.

Did the lesson help you with your accuracy in reading this story? _____

Now, choose the phrase below that, in your opinion, describes how much the lesson on pronunciation might help you read with better accuracy in the future?

   not at all   maybe a little   sometimes   probably often   a lot—a big difference

Finally, describe your plan for reading with more accuracy in the future. For example, what will you do when you encounter a word you don't know how to say?

_____

_____

Name _____ Date _____

Phrases

Read these phrases to yourself as you listen to them being read aloud.

be back before <u>sunlight</u>	the place is <u>bare</u>	<u>lock</u> us in this <u>cage</u>
<u>lock</u> us up	put the <u>locking</u> <u>device</u> on	<u>hadn't</u> <u>locked</u> it
look at the <u>chain</u>	<u>knocked</u> over his <u>coffee</u>	<u>merely</u> sitting in their <u>cage</u>
<u>stroke</u> of luck	it was too <u>weak</u>	a couple of <u>ordinary</u> toys
no, <u>sorry</u>	two <u>monkeys</u>	that's <u>odd</u>
'Mr. <u>Monkey</u> <u>Police</u>'	a strange <u>species</u>	

Could you read every word? If not, repeat reading and listening until you can. Then, try reading the phrases on your own without listening.

Story

Read the story to yourself as you listen to it being read aloud. Repeat reading and listening until you know every word.

It was Friday night. The zoo was closed and the keeper had gone home. **Two monkeys**, Ned and Ellie, were **merely sitting in their cage** when Ellie said, "You know, people must not be that bright. They **lock us in this cage**, and except for **a couple of ordinary toys** that would only interest a baby, **the place is bare**. Don't they realize that we chimps are much smarter than that? I'm bored!"

Ned was only half listening because he was staring at the door. "**That's odd**," he said.

"What's odd? People? That's what I have been saying. They are **a strange species**. I've heard that after they **lock us up** for the night, they go home and lock themselves up for the night!"

"**No, sorry**. That's not what I'm talking about. **Look at the chain** around the door. I think **'Mr. Monkey Police'** forgot to **put the locking device on**. It's amazing how easily humans can get distracted. He probably **knocked over his coffee** or just thought **it was too weak** and that was enough to make him forget that he **hadn't locked it**. What a **stroke of luck** for us!"

"What do you mean? Do you want to leave?"

"Why not? You were just complaining that this place is no castle. We could just roam around for a while and **be back before sunlight**. When the keepers come, they'll never know. We'll just be sitting here looking like the dumb monkeys they think we are."

"Now that would be amusing!" said Ellie. "Let's go!"

Name _____ Date _____

On Your Own

Think about how the word *lock* is used in each of these phrases from the story. First, underline whether it is a noun (naming word), a verb (doing word), or an adjective (describing word).

1.	lock us in this cage	noun	verb	adjective
2.	lock us up for the night	noun	verb	adjective
3.	put the locking device on	noun	verb	adjective
4.	hadn't locked it	noun	verb	adjective
5.	open the lock	noun	verb	adjective

Now, in your notebook or journal, write three sentences using *lock* or one of its forms. Make one use *lock* as a noun, one as a verb, and one as an adjective.

Story Questions Main Idea, Making Inferences, Vocabulary, Critical Thinking

Think about the story you listened to and practiced on page 65. Now, find out how well you understood it! Answer the questions below. You may need to go back and read the story again.

1. Think about what this story is about, or its main idea. Then, write a good a title for it. _____

2. What is Ellie's chief complaint about living at the zoo?
   A. The monkeys never get to go out of their cages.
   B. The people stare at them all day.
   C. The keeper doesn't pay enough attention to them.
   D. The toys are too simple and she is bored.

3. Which of the following statements is not true?
   A. Ned and Ellie both think humans are not all that smart.
   B. Ned and Ellie both like the idea of roaming around the zoo.
   C. Ned and Ellie both want to escape for good.
   D. Ned and Ellie are both monkeys who live in a zoo.

4. Which of the following is the correct pronunciation of the word **species** (a variety of animal)?
   A. spē shĕs   C. spĕ shēs
   B. spē shēz   D. spĕ shēz

5. What did Ellie mean by her comment that the people go home and lock themselves up for the night?

   _____

   _____

   _____

Name _____ Date _____

Reading with Expression—Pitch and Volume

Sentences, paragraphs, and stories are interesting only when they are read with expression. A robot reads each word the same—flat and without feeling. People express different moods and feelings by changing the pitch of their voices—going higher or lower for certain words. For example, you can use a higher pitch to highlight a word. Read this sentence. Make your voice go higher on the underlined words:

Except for a couple of ordinary toys that would only interest a <u>baby</u>, this place is <u>bare</u>.

In this sentence, the words *baby* and *bare* are important, so you stress them by raising the pitch of your voice. Sometimes in a sentence, though, a certain word is *very* important. Just raising the pitch a little bit isn't quite enough. To stress very important words, you can turn up the **volume**. Volume means loudness. The sentence is written below with different words in all capital letters. Read each one saying the word in all capitals louder than the rest.

I think 'Mr. Monkey Police' forgot to PUT the locking device on.

I think 'MR. MONKEY POLICE' forgot to put the locking device on.

Which one expresses what Ned is thinking and feeling in the story? The very important part is *Mr. Monkey Police*, because Ned is making fun of his human keeper. To read with expression, sometimes you have to adjust the loudness of your voice as well as the pitch. Now, read the sentence once more. Make your pitch go higher on the underlined word and your volume go up on the part in all capitals.

I think 'MR. MONKEY POLICE' forgot to put the <u>locking</u> device on.

Try It!

Now, use what you learned about highlighting words by adjusting the pitch or volume of your voice. Read the sentences below. Think about which words should be stressed by just raising the pitch. Are there any very important words—important enough to turn up the volume of your voice as well? Work with a partner to experiment. Take turns reading the sentences different ways by changing the pitch or volume of your voice on certain words. Decide together how to read the sentences with the best expression. Then, practice and be prepared if your teacher asks you to read aloud to the class.

1. "What's odd? People? That's what I have been saying. They are a strange species. I've heard that after they lock us up for the night, they go home and lock themselves up for the night!"

2. "It's amazing how easily humans can get distracted. He probably knocked over his coffee or just thought it was too weak and that was enough to make him forget that he hadn't locked it. What a stroke of luck for us!"

Name _____ Date _____

🏁 Fluency Checkpoint

In the box below, the story has been rewritten as a reader's theater script. Work with two other students to prepare for presenting the story as reader's theater. First, you need someone to read the parts of the story that are not spoken directly by one of the characters—a narrator. Then, you need someone to read the parts of Ned and Ellie. Take turns reading different parts. Then, decide who will take each speaking part for the presentation. Use a highlighter to mark your part. Then, practice reading the script together until you are all ready to perform. Remember, a reader's theater is *read*, not memorized or acted out. To do a good job, you each must be able to read your part fluently—accurately, at a good pace, and with excellent expression. (Use the direction words in *italics* to help you read the parts with expression.) After your oral presentation, your teacher will evaluate your performance for fluency.

Narrator:	It was Friday night. The zoo was closed and the keeper had gone home. Two monkeys, Ned and Ellie, were merely sitting in their cage.
Ellie:	(*complaining*) You know, people must not be that bright. They lock us in this cage, and except for a couple of ordinary toys that would only interest a baby, the place is bare. Don't they realize that we chimps are much smarter than that? I'm bored!
Narrator:	Ned was only half listening because he was staring at the door.
Ned:	(*pondering softly to himself*) That's odd . . .
Ellie:	(*answering, then rambling on*) "What's odd? People? *That's* what I have been saying. They are a strange species. I've heard that after they lock us up for the night, they go home and lock *themselves* up for the night!"
Ned:	(*realizing he hadn't been paying attention to Ellie*) No, sorry. That's not what I'm talking about. (*hushed, as if letting Ellie in on a secret*) Look at the chain around the door. (*sarcastically*) I think 'Mr. Monkey Police' forgot to put the locking device on. It's amazing how easily humans can get distracted. He probably knocked over his coffee or just thought it was too weak and that was enough to make him forget that he hadn't locked it. (*delighted*) What a stroke of luck for us!
Ellie:	(*shocked*) What do you mean? Do you want to *leave*?
Ned:	(*confidently*) Why not? You were just complaining that this place is no castle. We could just roam around for a while and be back before sunlight. When the keepers come, they'll never know. (*with exaggerated innocence*) We'll just be sitting here looking like the dumb monkeys they think we are."
Ellie:	(*in pleased agreement*) "Now *that* would be amusing! Let's go!

Write the names of the people in your group who are reading each part:

Narrator: _____ Ellie: _____ Ned: _____

Name _____ Date _____

Phrases

Read these phrases to yourself as you listen to them being read aloud.

sort of <u>accident</u>	<u>whenever</u> they got	had <u>invited</u> Dave
<u>lies</u> <u>twisted</u>	<u>lying</u> at the bottom	find something <u>valuable</u>
<u>reminded</u> them	the pirates <u>captured</u>	go down in <u>flames</u>
<u>diving</u> for lost treasure	<u>grinned</u> as he thought	could <u>manage</u>
a <u>mighty</u> pirate ship	no <u>doubt</u>	a <u>chest</u> filled with gold
to <u>pilot</u> the boat	sat in <u>silence</u>	in low <u>tide</u>
<u>sang</u> out	<u>gradually</u> made its way	<u>tossed</u> in a storm

Story

Read the story to yourself as you listen to it being read aloud. Repeat reading and listening until you know every word.

The two men had been friends for 20 years. Old Jim had a map to a spot where **a mighty pirate ship** was thought to have sunk. **Whenever they got** together, the men talked of someday **diving for lost treasure**. Now, they were actually doing it.

With map in hand, Old Jim had rented a boat and **had invited Dave** along. Jim had been a sailor and so was able **to pilot the boat**. Dave had taught diving to tourists. If anyone **could manage** to **find something valuable lying at the bottom** of the ocean, it would **no doubt** be these two.

With Old Jim at the helm, the boat **gradually made its way** toward the spot. Dave **sat in silence**. He **grinned as he thought** about finding **a chest filled with gold** and jewels. People said they were crazy. But, Dave **reminded them** it had been done before. In 1985, a treasure hunter found a ship named *Atocha* with millions of dollars worth of gold and silver. Old Jim's map could be real. They were finally going to find out.

According to the map, they were looking for a pirate ship named *Silver Lady* that went down in 1608. Dave let his mind drift over the waves of the sea. "What wonderful treasure had **the pirates captured**? What might have happened to the *Silver Lady* and her crew? Did the pirates run aground **in low tide**? Did they have some other **sort of accident**? Did the ship get hit by a flash of lightning, catch on fire, and **go down in flames**? Was the ship **tossed in a storm** and what's left of the *Silver Lady* **lies twisted** on the ocean floor?"

"Dave! Up ahead! Look!" Old Jim's voice **sang out**, snapping Dave back into reality.

"What? What is it?" he called back, shaking off his daydream.

"I see something," he answered slowly with a mixture of excitement and fear.

Dave got up. He grabbed the binoculars. He skimmed the ocean's surface.

"Oh my gosh," he barely managed to whisper out loud. "It can't be . . . ."

Lesson 15 *(cont.)*

Name _____ Date _____

On Your Own

Some words used in this story have more than one meaning. The only way to tell the correct meaning is using the context, or the words around it. Find each word below in the story. Reread the sentence in which it appears. Then, underline the meaning of the word as it is used in this story.

spot:	1) a small round mark	2) a particular place
lying:	1) saying something untrue	2) resting undisturbed
pilot:	1) person who flies a plane	2) steer a ship
chest:	1) upper front of the body	2) trunk or storage box
mind:	1) to watch over for a time	2) thoughts, ideas, and perceptions
skimmed:	1) removed a layer from the top	2) looked over quickly
manage:	1) keep control of	2) achieve something difficult

Now, in your journal or on a fresh sheet of paper, use these words in sentences in which each word has the first meaning listed above.

Story Questions Main Idea, Identifying Purpose, Vocabulary, Critical Thinking

Think about the story you listened to and practiced on page 69. Now, find out how well you understood it! Answer the questions below. You may need to go back and read the story again.

1. Which of these would be the best title for this story?
   A. A Pirate's Life   C. Hunting for Sunken Treasure
   B. The Silver Lady   D. Old Jim's Map

2. Which of these did Dave not say could be the cause of the sinking of *Silver Lady*?
   A. She was captured.   C. She ran aground in low tide.
   B. She caught fire.   D. She had an accident.

3. Which of the following shows an incorrect meaning for the term?
   A. helm: the part of a boat where it is steered
   B. binoculars: a device that makes distant things appear larger
   C. drift: a wave of cool air that makes one feel uncomfortable
   D. run aground: to strike or get stuck on the bottom of shallow water

4. Do you think the men had a good chance of finding the *Silver Lady*? Why or why not?

   _____

   _____

#50279—Increasing Fluency with High Frequency Word Phrases   © *Shell Education*

Name _____ Date _____

Reading with Expression—Creating Suspense with Dialogue

Of course, saying the right words when reading is important. But, how you say them makes the difference between grabbing your listeners' attention and losing their interest. The mood in the first part of the story you just read is calm and puts the readers at ease. Then, all of a sudden, the mood switches unexpectedly. Look back at the story. At what point does the mood suddenly switch? Up to that point, the author is telling a story about two men. Then, the writer switches to a different style—dialogue. Suddenly, the men themselves speak. It is almost as if we have been watching the story from a distance and then are thrown into the scene as it happened. Look at the dialogue. The words the men say are nothing special. It is how they say the words that creates the mood. Read this sentence below without any feeling or expression: ***I see something.*** Does it make you want to know what I see? Not really. Now read it as if you were scared and nervous and didn't want the "something" to hear you. Read it again. This time imagine that what you see is a wonderful surprise and you shout with joy. Finally, read it as if you are not sure if it is a good thing or a bad thing that you see—curious but cautious.

The writer of this story uses dialogue to create suspense. When you read the characters' words, you put in the feeling and expression yourself, rather than just being told how they felt. Compare these two ways of saying the same thing. One is ho-hum. The other creates suspense.

Old Jim told Dave to look up ahead. Dave wondered what it was he was to look at.

"Dave! Up ahead! Look!" Old Jim's voice sang out. "What? What is it?" he called back.

Try It!

Now, have some fun creating different moods with dialogue. Below is the dialogue from the story. Think about what Dave might have seen through the binoculars that he thinks is unbelievable. All we know is that it is something unexpected. Is it something wonderful, scary, amazing, horrifying, or . . . ? Use your imagination. Then, read the dialogue with a partner several times. Each time read it to express a different feeling based on the reaction to what they see.

Old Jim:	Dave! Up ahead! Look!
Dave:	What? What is it?
Old Jim:	I see something.
Dave:	Oh my gosh! It can't be . . .

Name _____ Date _____

 # Fluency Checkpoint

You have already listened to, practiced, and read the story below. Now it's time to check your reading fluency. Remember, fluency means not just getting the words right, but also reading at a good rate and with expression, or feeling. Reread the story again, as if you were rehearsing it for a performance. Repeat this as many times as necessary so that you can read it fluently.

The two men had been friends for 20 years. Old Jim had a map to a spot where a mighty pirate ship was thought to have sunk. Whenever they got together, the men talked of someday diving for lost treasure. Now, they were actually doing it.

With map in hand, Old Jim had rented a boat and had invited Dave along. Jim had been a sailor and so was able to pilot the boat. Dave had taught diving to tourists. If anyone could manage to find something valuable lying at the bottom of the ocean, it would no doubt be these two.

With Old Jim at the helm, the boat gradually made its way toward the spot. Dave sat in silence. He grinned as he thought about finding a chest filled with gold and jewels. People said they were crazy. But, Dave reminded them it had been done before. In 1985, a treasure hunter found a ship named *Atocha* with millions of dollars worth of gold and silver. Old Jim's map could be real. They were finally going to find out.

According to the map, they were looking for a pirate ship named *Silver Lady* that went down in 1608. Dave let his mind drift over the waves of the sea. "What wonderful treasure had the pirates captured? What might have happened to the *Silver Lady* and her crew? Did the pirates run aground in low tide? Did they have some other sort of accident? Did the ship get hit by a flash of lightning, catch on fire, and go down in flames? Was the ship tossed in a storm and what's left of the *Silver Lady* lies twisted on the ocean floor?"

"Dave! Up ahead! Look!" Old Jim's voice sang out, snapping Dave back into reality.

"What? What is it?" he called back, shaking off his daydream.

"I see something," he answered slowly with a mixture of excitement and fear.

Dave got up. He grabbed the binoculars. He skimmed the ocean's surface.

"Oh my gosh," he barely managed to whisper out loud. "It can't be . . . "

Evaluation

Think back over this lesson and look over the story one more time. What can you use as clues to help you figure out how to read with good expression? One is given below. Write two more.

1. <u>Punctuation marks help signal how something should be read.</u>

2. _____

3. _____

Name _____ Date _____

Phrases

Read these phrases to yourself as you listen to them being read aloud.

introducing to you   had great success   respect Galileo's research

could be mentioned   only scratched the surface   out of the darkness

scientific research   by the light of a candle   several telescopes

concept of gravity   definitions given to him   far into the depth of space

larger than normal   refused to accept   how the physical world operates

he constructed   take for granted   imagine Galileo's excitement

Nonfiction for Divided Reading

Read along to yourself as you listen to the whole article read aloud. Then, your teacher will assign you one or more of the parts to learn to read fluently. You will be reading your part or parts together with one or more other students. You will also need to read the parts labeled "All."

Repeat reading and listening until you know every word in your part. Later, you will be performing it as part of a group choral reading.

R1: Today we are going to take a trip back in time. We'll meet some great pioneers of science who lived in the 1500–1600s. This time is known as the Renaissance— a time of change and rebirth.

R2: Much of the science we **take for granted** is the direct result of great thinkers at this time. They **refused to accept** the explanations for things. **By the light of a candle**, these men led the world **out of the darkness** of misunderstanding. Though many **could be mentioned**,

All: *We are **introducing to you** just two—Galileo and Newton.*

R3: Galileo was born in Italy in 1564. From an early age, he was interested in **how the physical world operates**.

R4: Rather than just accepting the **definitions given to him** in school, Galileo wanted to test and observe things for himself. Since one can't see time or space, Galileo wanted to find ways to learn more about these things.

All: *There must be more than meets the eye.*

R5: Galileo designed **several telescopes**. One **he constructed** could make objects appear 32 times **larger than normal**. People in the shipping business loved it. But, Galileo aimed it at the heavens.

R6: At the time, many people believed that Earth was at the center of the universe and that everything in space revolved around us. **Imagine Galileo's excitement** when he discovered moons orbiting the planet Jupiter instead–moons too small to see without a telescope.

Name _____ Date _____

Nonfiction for Divided Reading *(cont.)*

All: *Although we respect Galileo's research, he was punished for his efforts to correct the beliefs of most people at this time.*

R7: Fortunately, Galileo's work survived him. Since then, of course, we have built upon his ideas. We now have powerful telescopes that allow us to see **far into the depth of space**.

R9: As if to honor him, a craft named *Galileo* spent 14 years exploring space. It made 34 orbits of Jupiter—one of the planets Galileo first observed with his own telescopes.

R10: Just months after Galileo's death in 1642, another well-known scientific thinker was born.

All: *Isaac Newton.*

R11: Perhaps you have heard the story of how an apple fell from a tree that he was sitting under. It hit him on the head, and *tah-dah*, he figured out gravity.

R12: Amusing, but it wasn't quite that simple. In fact, the **concept of gravity** was already known. The questions were: If the moon goes around Earth, was it Earth's gravity that held it in orbit? Gravity can cause an apple to fall, but is it strong enough to hold the moon in place?

R13: Newton answered those questions. But that **only scratched the surface**. He took it further. He was able to calculate the exact force needed to hold various bodies in their paths. He **had great success**. He shared his ideas about orbits, ellipses, and traveling objects with his friend, Halley.

All: *Halley ran with that idea and ended up with a comet named after him.*

R14: Unlike Galileo, Newton's research was accepted immediately in Britain where he lived.

R15: Within the next 50 years, **scientific research** of all sorts began to be accepted as fact.

All: *The world was changing.*

R16: Science and technology grew from bud to blossom quickly. The world was open to discovery and invention. Faith and fact began to find a way to exist together. Today, science and technology continue to help us live better and understand our world.

All: *Thanks to people like Galileo and Newton who planted the seeds.*

On Your Own

In this lesson, you must work together as a team. Each of you will have equal responsibility for preparing to read your part in the reading. Before you begin, pledge to contribute the best you can to the team effort by signing your name on the line.

_____

As a team, practice reading your part together until you can do it smoothly.

Name _____ Date _____

 # Questions

Think about the article you listened to and practiced on pages 73–74. Now, find out how well you understood it! Answer the questions below. You may need to go back and read the article again.

1. Which statement best describes the main idea of the article?
   A. Galileo and Newton are the most important people in scientific history.
   B. Galileo and Newton are among those who led the way for technology development.
   C. Newton's friend Halley has a comet named after him.
   D. Before Galileo and Newton, people knew nothing about science.

2. Which of the following statements is not a fact drawn from the article?
   A. Galileo died just before Newton was born.
   B. At Galileo's time, most people believed that Earth was the center of the universe.
   C. As soon as Galileo published his research, people realized that there were other planets.
   D. Galileo observed objects in space using a telescope he designed and made himself.

3. What does the word *physical* mean as it is used by Reader 3?
   A. part of and existing in the real world
   B. a general examination of one's health
   C. having to do with the body or bodily strength
   D. None of the above

4. This article was about two scientific thinkers of the Renaissance period—Galileo and Newton. Based only on the information given in the article, which of the two do you think made the more important contribution to science and why?

   _____

   _____

   _____

Extra Credit Bonus: Explain what each of these expressions means in the article.

1. These men led the world out of the darkness: _____

   _____

2. Newton answered the questions about gravity, but that only scratched the surface: _____

3. Science and technology grew from bud to blossom quickly: _____

   _____

Name _____ Date _____

 # Reading with Expression—Audience

Look at the list of words below. What do they have in common?

> whisper   shout   moan   growl   whine   snarl   cackle
> sob   state   ask   shriek   murmur   exclaim   demand

These are just some of the ways you can use your voice to give meaning to what you say. You can even use your voice to give a nonsense sentence feeling or emotion. Try it now. Read the nonsense sentence below in some of the ways described by the words above.

The snulak gleared smarfly.

You know by now that how you say the words when you read makes a big difference. But, even if you read the right words, at the right speed, and with good expression, you still may be missing an important thing to consider—the audience. After all, you are speaking with the expectation that someone will be listening!

When you are speaking or reading aloud, you need to check two things before you ever open your mouth to begin. First, how many people will be your listeners? Second, how close or far away will your audience be? Then, adjust the loudness of your voice so you can be heard by everyone. Practice reading the nonsense sentence above for different-size audiences: one person in a small room, a group of ten sitting on the floor in front of you, another fourth grade class at their seats in the classroom, and a group of 200 parents in an auditorium!

Try It!

You have been assigned and have been practicing your parts of the article on pages 73–74. You will be reading this aloud as a group. Now do two more things in final preparation. First, highlight the parts you will read for the final performance. Second, practice reading the parts on your own several times. Each time pretend that you have a different audience. Adjust the loudness of your voice to match these conditions.

1. Your audience is one person sitting with you in a small room.
2. Your audience is another fourth grade class sitting at their seats in the classroom.
3. Your audience is parents at back-to-school night—200 of them in an auditorium.
4. Your audience is a group of ten kids sitting on the floor in front of you in the library.

Evaluation

You are going to perform a choral reading of the article. Your teacher will choose an audience for your final presentation. You will read your assigned parts along with your group. Be sure you know your parts and where to come in. Remember to match your volume to the size of your audience. Your teacher will listen and evaluate each section's preparation and reading fluency.

Name _____ Date _____

 ## Phrases

Read these phrases to yourself as you listen to them being read aloud.

with my dad's <u>camera</u>	<u>Bent</u> Branch Camp	<u>fifth</u> graders
<u>headed</u> up the hill	<u>extremely</u> glad	in every <u>conversation</u>
every <u>practical</u> reason	I <u>sighed</u>	stuck in <u>traffic</u>
<u>burst</u> into cheers	some <u>mammals</u> hiding	in <u>Australia</u>
in <u>Virginia</u>	in a <u>pine</u> forest	on a <u>mission</u>
<u>wandering</u> through the trees	a few <u>pine</u> trees	my <u>mission</u>
<u>dragging</u> all our stuff	in the <u>territory</u>	got the <u>nerve</u>
gave me the <u>drill</u>	<u>troops</u> of fourth	

A Narrative Essay

Read the essay to yourself as you listen to it being read aloud. Repeat reading and listening until you know every word.

I was **on a mission**. As soon as I heard about it, I wanted to go on the summer campout. I begged my parents day and night. I brought it up **in every conversation**. I gave them **every practical reason** I could think of for why they should send me to camp. Finally, after I promised to do extra chores for a year, they gave in.

On the day we left, excited **troops of fourth** and **fifth graders** loaded onto the bus. But, after an hour had passed, we were still in the city **stuck in traffic**. The mood changed from excitement to restlessness. We all just wanted to get there and start having some fun! Finally, we broke free and **headed up the hill** away from the city. Another two hours passed, but at least we were getting somewhere. While traveling on a single lane road, someone noticed a small sign that said ***Bent Branch Camp*** *2 miles*. The whole bus **burst into cheers**. A lot of kids were hungry and I had to go to the bathroom. I was **extremely glad** that we would be there soon.

The bus came to a stop. We wondered why. There was nothing there—no people, no buildings, and, most worrisome for me, no bathroom. "Here we are, boys!" the driver said happily as he opened the bus door. We filed out **dragging all our stuff**. I was especially careful **with my dad's camera**. He **gave me the drill** about responsibility.

The campground was **in a pine forest in Virginia**, but it might as well have been **in Australia**. Besides **a few pine trees** and probably **some mammals hiding** in them, we were the only living things **in the territory**. Remembering my urgent problem, **I sighed**. I **got the nerve** to tell my camp leader and he sent me off **wandering through the trees** for a private spot.

A little while later, we made a campfire. When the sun went down, we told stories by moonlight. The next day we went on a hike. Then, there were fun activities every day. When we first arrived, I thought I had made a huge mistake coming to camp. But, once we were settled in, the rest of the trip was a blast. It turns out that **my mission** was a success. Now, how am I going to convince my parents to let me go again next year?

 **Lesson 17** *(cont.)*

Name _____ Date _____

On Your Own

English is filled with expressions—sayings that mean something other than exactly what the words say. For example, the essay says that they were stuck in traffic. Of course, the kids were not caught under the wheels of cars. The expression here means *delayed because there were many cars*. Below are four more expressions used in the essay. Find each one and reread the sentence in which it appears. Then, on the lines below, write what each expression really means as it is used in the article.

1. we **broke free** _____

2. bus **burst into cheers** _____

3. he **gave me the drill** _____

4. the trip was **a blast** _____

Essay Questions Main Idea, Details, Vocabulary, Critical Thinking

Think about the essay you listened to and practiced on page 77. Now find out how well you understood it! Answer the questions below. You may need to go back and read the essay again.

1. Which of these sentences best summarizes the main point of the essay?
   A. Despite a disappointing start, the writer ended up making a good choice by going to camp.
   B. If you try hard enough, you might be able to convince your parents to agree to something.
   C. The boys were not well prepared for going on the trip.
   D. Fourth and fifth graders get impatient when they have to wait a long time.

2. This essay has five paragraphs. Which of these statements are correct?
   A. The first paragraph introduces the topic.
   B. The last paragraph is the conclusion and ties back to the first paragraph.
   C. The three middle paragraphs give details about the topic.
   D. All of the above.

3. Which pair of words below do not mean the same or almost the same thing?
   A. convince—persuade   C. restlessness—patience
   B. practical—sensible   D. mission—task

4. These statements were not directly given in the story. Figure out if they are true or false. Write T or F.
   A. The children lived in a city in or near the state of Virginia. _____
   B. The trip was for boys aged 9–11. _____
   C. The bus trip took at least three hours. _____
   D. The camp leader was the father of the boy writing the story. _____

 #50279—*Increasing Fluency with High Frequency Word Phrases*   © *Shell Education*

Name _____ Date _____

 # Reading with Expression—Eye-Voice Span

When you are walking, running, or riding a bike, are you looking at your feet? No, you are looking at what is ahead of you! You depend on your eyes to tell you what is coming up before you actually get there.

Your eyes work much faster than your feet. They also work faster than your voice. Think of reading like walking, running, or riding a bike. As you are saying a word, your eyes should be looking ahead to see what is coming up.

How far ahead? That depends on the difficulty of what you are reading. If the words are familiar, your path ahead should be clear. You should be able to see several words beyond where you are. If the text has some new or unfamiliar terms, there may be some bumps in the road that slow you down. However, if you preview those bumps before you actually get there, you may be able to get over them without stopping or tripping on them.

Try to look at phrases or chunks of words ahead of where you are reading.

You may be surprised / at how good / your eyes are / at letting you know / and preparing you / for what is coming up.

Try It!

Read sentences 1–5 in chunks. As your voice is saying one chunk, use your eyes to preread the next chunk before you get there.

1. The campground / was a pine forest / in Virginia.
2. On the day we left / excited troops of fourth and fifth graders / loaded onto the bus.
3. There was nothing there / no people / no buildings / and most worrisome for me / no bathroom.
4. A little while later / we pitched our tents / and made a campfire.
5. Finally / we broke free / and headed up the hill / away from the city.

Now, divide these two longer sentences into meaningful chunks. Draw a (**/**) between the chunks.

6. Then there were fun activities every day for the rest of the week.
7. Besides a few pine trees and probably some mammals hiding in them we were the only living things in the territory.

 The next time you are asked to read something, use what you have learned about looking ahead at what is coming up. As you are reading one chunk, let your eyes check out the next chunk before you get there.

Name _____ Date _____

Fluency Checkpoint

You have already listened to, practiced, and read the essay below. Now it's time to check your reading fluency. Remember, fluency means not just getting the words right, but also reading at a good rate and with expression, or feeling. Reread the essay again, as if you were rehearsing it for a performance. Repeat this as many times as necessary so that you can read it fluently.

I was on a mission. As soon as I heard about it, I wanted to go on the summer campout. I begged my parents day and night. I brought it up in every conversation. I gave them every practical reason I could think of for why they should send me to camp. Finally, after I promised to do extra chores for a year, they gave in.

On the day we left, excited troops of fourth and fifth graders loaded onto the bus. But, after an hour had passed, we were still in the city stuck in traffic. The mood changed from excitement to restlessness. We all just wanted to get there and start having some fun! Finally, we broke free and headed up the hill away from the city. Another two hours passed, but at least we were getting somewhere. While traveling on a single lane road, someone noticed a small sign that said *Bent Branch Camp 2 miles*. The whole bus burst into cheers. A lot of kids were hungry and I had to go to the bathroom. I was extremely glad that we would be there soon.

The bus came to a stop. We wondered why. There was nothing there—no people, no buildings, and, most worrisome for me, no bathroom. "Here we are, boys!" the driver said happily as he opened the bus door. We filed out dragging all our stuff. I was especially careful with my dad's camera. He gave me the drill about responsibility.

The campground was in a pine forest in Virginia, but it might as well have been in Australia. Besides a few pine trees and probably some mammals hiding in them, we were the only living things in the territory. Remembering my urgent problem, I sighed. I got the nerve to tell my camp leader and he sent me off wandering through the trees for a private spot.

A little while later, we made a campfire. When the sun went down, we told stories by moonlight. The next day we went on a hike. Then, there were fun activities every day. When we first arrived, I thought I had made a huge mistake coming to camp. But, once we were settled in, the rest of the trip was a blast. It turns out that my mission was a success. Now, how am I going to convince my parents to let me go again next year?

Evaluation

If you could change one thing about your reading, what would it be?_____

_____

_____

Name _____ Date _____

Phrases

Read these phrases to yourself as you listen to them being read aloud.

in <u>southeast</u> <u>Mississippi</u>	one <u>Saturday</u> evening	I <u>haven't</u> missed
a <u>canoe</u> trip	to <u>celebrate</u>	<u>trace</u> the tracks
<u>pretended</u> to be	my joy turned to <u>pain</u>	riding our <u>bicycles</u>
<u>aren't</u> going	special <u>relationship</u>	by the old <u>pasture</u>
bring our <u>boots</u>	look for <u>evidence</u>	the "<u>explorer</u>" hat
in their <u>pen</u>	already <u>lonely</u>	move to <u>Chicago</u>
my <u>grandmother</u>	when Dad <u>spoke</u>	with a fishing <u>net</u>
beavers build <u>dams</u>	a much better <u>income</u>	in my <u>throat</u>

A Personal Essay

Read the essay to yourself as you listen to it being read aloud. Repeat reading and listening until you know every word.

I grew up in Wiggins—a town **in southeast Mississippi**. When I was a little kid, my grandparents lived with us. **My grandmother** took care of us while my parents worked. It was my grandfather, though, that provided the fun. In our house, when you reached the age of four, Grandpa gave you a special hat. Mine was red. Receiving **the "explorer" hat** meant that you were old enough to start going with Grandpa on his famous explorations of the world outside the house. The first time I proudly wore my hat was on a trip to a nearby farm to see some new piglets **in their pen**.

In spring, we'd go to the pond **by the old pasture**. Grandpa had us **bring our boots** so we could tromp around in the mud. We'd **trace the tracks** of animals that drank at the pond or **look for evidence** of what kinds of birds visited there. The best thing, however, was looking for tadpoles. We'd reach out **with a fishing net** to scoop some up. We would put them in a bucket and look at them closely.

By the time I was six, we were **riding our bicycles** to Black Creek. I remember Grandpa pointing out a big pile of sticks and explaining how **beavers build dams**. Another time, when I was seven, we took **a canoe trip** on one of the bigger streams. We **pretended to be** native Choctaw Indians

One Saturday evening when I was eight, we were having a special family dinner **to celebrate** that my dad had gotten a new job with **a much better income**. We were going to **move to Chicago**! But **my joy turned to pain when Dad spoke**. "Grandma and Grandpa **aren't going** with us," he said. His words stuck **in my throat**. We had a very **special relationship** with Grandpa. I couldn't imagine being without him. I was **already lonely** just thinking about it.

Later that year, we did move to Chicago. Grandma and Grandpa come to visit as often as they can. It's great to see them, but our lives have changed. Not one day has gone by when **I haven't missed** our time together back in Wiggins.

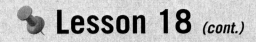

Name _____ Date _____

On Your Own

What's the difference between *you're* and *your*? Yes, one has an apostrophe. More importantly, the one with the apostrophe is a contraction meaning *you are*. The other one means *belongs to you*.

Write the contractions for these words. (Hint: They are all in the story.)

1. we would: _____

2. could not: _____

3. are not: _____

4. it is: _____

5. have not: _____

Essay Questions Main Idea, Sequence, Vocabulary, Critical Thinking

Think about the essay you listened to and practiced on page 81. Now find out how well you understood it! Answer the questions below. You may need to go back and read the essay again.

1. Which of these statements best tells the main point the writer is trying to make?

   A. Growing up with his grandparents at home was a special experience.

   B. Families should not move away from their grandparents.

   C. Chicago is a long way from Mississippi.

   D. Sometimes both parents have to work.

2. Write First, Second, Third, and Fourth on the lines to show the order that the events happened.

   _____ The author took a canoe trip with Grandpa.

   _____ The family moved away from the grandparents.

   _____ The author got a red "explorer" hat from Grandpa.

   _____ The author watched tadpoles grow into frogs.

3. Compound words are made by putting two words together to make a new word. To be a compound, the original words must be able to stand alone. Which of the following words in **bold** is *not* a compound word?

   A. I grew up in Wiggins—a town in **southeast** Mississippi.

   B. My **grandmother** took care of us while my parents worked.

   C. The best thing, however, was looking for **tadpoles**.

4. The story you read is both happy and sad. Do you think it is more happy or more sad? Explain why you think as you do.

   _____

   _____

   _____

Name _____ Date _____

 # Reading with Expression—Signal Words and Phrases

Did you know that your brain works faster than any computer? It is so fast that sometimes it gives you information that you are not even aware has arrived. For example, if you put your hand on a hot stove, you will pull it away instantly—you might say, "without thinking." Actually, you are thinking, but your brain delivered the message so fast that you didn't realize it until after you moved your hand. Your remarkable brain learns to recognize all kinds of information—not just things that might harm you. It responds to signals from inside your body and from everything around you.

When you read, your brain is working along with your eyes to make sense of what you see. At first, learning to read is hard work. But, once you have taught your brain to recognize the signals that go along with reading, it will respond without you having to "think" about it.

Some words and phrases can be helpful signals for your brain to learn. These words and phrases give you clues about what is important or what is coming next. Here are a few examples:

Next, (more is coming)

First, (things are coming in an order)

such as (example is coming)

Most of all, (most important thing is coming next)

In insertion (something will be inserted on)

However, (something is changing)

After (telling when)

because (a reason is coming)

in between, (telling where)

Finally, (this is the last thing)

Try It!

Several signal words and phrases appear in the essay you read. Some are shown in bold type below. First, find the sentence in which each appears. Think about what signal it is giving. Next, complete each sentence below with a new, different ending of your own.

1. **When I was** a little kid, _____ .
2. **Eventually,** _____ .
3. **By the time** I was six, _____ .
4. **One Saturday evening,** _____ .

Now, write a short summary of the story. Use the signal words to help you put the events in order.

First, _____ .

Next, _____ .

Then, _____ .

Finally, _____ .

Name _____ Date _____

 Fluency Checkpoint

You have already listened to, practiced, and read the essay below. Now it's time to check your reading fluency. Remember, fluency means not just getting the words right, but also reading at a good rate and with expression, or feeling. Reread the essay again, as if you were rehearsing it for a performance. Repeat this as many times as necessary so that you can read it fluently.

> I grew up in Wiggins—a town in southeast Mississippi. When I was a little kid, my grandparents lived with us. My grandmother took care of us while my parents worked. It was my grandfather, though, that provided the fun. In our house, when you reached the age of four, Grandpa gave you a special hat. Mine was red. Receiving the "explorer" hat meant that you were old enough to start going with Grandpa on his famous explorations of the world outside the house. The first time I proudly wore my hat was on a trip to a nearby farm to see some new piglets in their pen.
>
> In spring, we'd go to the pond by the old pasture. Grandpa had us bring our boots so we could tromp around in the mud. We'd trace the tracks of animals that drank at the pond or look for evidence of what kinds of birds visited there. The best thing, however, was looking for tadpoles. We'd reach out with a fishing net to scoop some up. We would put them in a bucket and look at them closely.
>
> By the time I was six, we were riding our bicycles to Black Creek. I remember Grandpa pointing out a big pile of sticks and explaining how beavers build dams. Another time, when I was seven, we took a canoe trip on one of the bigger streams. We pretended to be native Choctaw Indians
>
> One Saturday evening when I was eight, we were having a special family dinner to celebrate that my dad had gotten a new job with a much better income. We were going to move to Chicago! But my joy turned to pain when Dad spoke. "Grandma and Grandpa aren't going with us," he said. His words stuck in my throat. We had a very special relationship with Grandpa. I couldn't imagine being without him. I was already lonely just thinking about it.
>
> Later that year, we did move to Chicago. Grandma and Grandpa come to visit as often as they can. It's great to see them, but our lives have changed. Not one day has gone by when I haven't missed our time together back in Wiggins.

Evaluation

Write one sentence that summarizes how you feel about your oral reading fluency. Remember, fluency means *accuracy* (getting the words right), *rate* (a good pace), and *expression* (with feeling).

_____

_____

Name _____ Date _____

Phrases

Read these phrases to yourself as you listen to them being read aloud.

it was <u>impossible</u>	the big <u>welcome</u> sign	after a <u>brief</u> conversation
the <u>remainder</u> of the week	in <u>truth</u>	<u>fierce</u> and <u>hated</u> rivals
yelled <u>aloud</u>	and his <u>cousin</u>	Ty <u>declared</u>
had trouble being <u>patient</u>	<u>scattered</u> around	schedule was <u>announced</u>
<u>tend</u> to look like this	a <u>couple</u> of hours	<u>football</u> fan
<u>snapped</u> the ball	packed some <u>sandwiches</u>	next <u>Sunday</u>

Story

Read the story to yourself as you listen to it being read aloud. Repeat reading and listening until you know every word.

Danny had always been a huge **football fan**. As soon as the fall **schedule was announced**, Danny marked on his calendar all the big games he wanted to watch. This year the New York Giants, his favorite team, were going to host their **fierce and hated rivals**—the Dallas Cowboys—the second week of October. Danny knew **it was impossible**, but he dreamed of being able to go to the game.

Then, one evening early in October, the phone rang. It was Danny's Uncle Alex. **After a brief conversation** about school and stuff, Uncle Alex said something that stunned Danny. Somehow Uncle Alex had gotten three tickets to the Dallas game and was inviting Danny to go to the game with him **and his cousin,** Ty. "Yahoo!" Danny **yelled aloud** after hanging up the phone. This was his dream come true! He could hardly wait for **next Sunday** to come!

The remainder of the week passed slowly and Danny **had trouble being patient**. But, finally, Sunday arrived. Uncle Alex and Ty picked Danny up early. They had **packed some sandwiches** and drinks because they knew they would have to spend **a couple of hours** in the parking lot before getting in. Danny's heart skipped a beat when he saw **the big welcome sign** in front of Giants' Stadium.

The stadium was enormous. Most people were wearing red and blue, but there were a few Dallas fans **scattered around**. When the Giants first **snapped the ball**, the crowd roared. **In truth**, Danny had never even imagined anything could be so loud!

Danny watched the game and had the time of his life. When Uncle Alex brought him back home late in the afternoon, Danny's mom asked how it was. However, Danny just stood there, speechless. His eyes beamed but no words came out. Finally, Ty answered for him. "He thought it was awesome," **Ty declared**. "He's looked like this for the last two hours. First-timers **tend to look like this**. But, don't worry. He'll probably come back down to earth in time for school tomorrow!"

 **Lesson 19** *(cont.)*

Name _____ Date _____

On Your Own

Synonyms are words that mean the same or almost the same thing. Good writers use synonyms to make their stories more exact and interesting. Below are some words used in the story. Write two synonyms for each. Tip: Need synonyms? Try a *thesaurus*—a reference book of synonyms.

Example: **remainder**:   rest   leftover

1. huge: _____   _____
2. brief: _____   _____
3. astounded: _____   _____
4. awesome: _____   _____

Story Questions Main Idea, Making Inferences, Vocabulary, Critical Thinking

Think about the story you listened to and practiced on page 85. You have read the story; now find out how well you understood it! Answer the questions below. You may need to go back and read the story again.

1. Which of these would be the best title for this story?
   A. A Fan's Dream Come True   C. The Giants vs. the Cowboys
   B. Uncle Alex Saves the Day   D. Being Patient Pays Off
2. Which of the following can you not tell from the story?
   A. The home team is the New York Giants.
   B. Danny never expected to be able to attend the game in person.
   C. The Giants' team colors include red and blue.
   D. Ty, Danny's cousin, is older than Danny.
3. Read these words from the story. Then write the number that matches the correct meaning.
   A. _____ fierce   1. said, stated
   B. _____ observed   2. looked at
   C. _____ tend   3. tough, aggressive
   D. _____ declared   4. generally or likely
4. One way to summarize a story is by answering the 5W questions. Think back to the story and answer the 5Ws:

Who? _____

What? _____

Where? _____

When? _____

Why? _____

Name _____ Date _____

 Reading with Expression—Showing Strong Feeling!

Have you ever been excited about something that happened and told someone else about the experience? When you told your story, your voice showed your feelings. Reading with expression means recreating the feelings associated with the written words. Sometimes you will be recreating the writer's feelings about something, such as a beautiful sunset, a scary moment, or a sad memory. Other times, you will be expressing the feelings of characters in a story. It is your job as the reader to figure out what feeling the words should show. For example, in the story "The Ugly Duckling," when the ducklings hatch, they exclaim, "How big the world is!" When they see that one of them is different looking, they say, "We don't want to play with him. He's ugly!" Later, when the ugly duckling has grown up, he sees a beautiful swan in the water and says, "I am so ugly!" But then, he realizes that he is seeing his own reflection and that he is not an ugly duckling, but a beautiful swan. He says, "I am a swan! This is almost too good to be true!"

Fortunately, when you are supposed to read something that expresses strong feeling, the writer usually gives you a signal called an exclamation point (**!**). When you see an exclamation point at the end of a word or sentence, you know it means that it should be said with strong feeling. Use the punctuation marks below as signals for how to read these statements:

Watch me.	No. I can't.	Stop it.	Come on.	Let's go.	We're #1.
Watch me!	No! I can't!	Stop it!	Come on!	Let's go!	We're #1!

Try It!

Now, use what you learned about expressing strong feeling and the use of an exclamation point as a signal for reading with strong feeling. Below are parts of the story you read, but they are missing some of the punctuation. Fill in a period (**.**) or exclamation point (**!**) to show how it should be read.

1. Somehow Uncle Alex had gotten three tickets to the Dallas game and was inviting Danny to go to the game with him and his cousin, Ty ( ) "Yahoo ( )" Danny yelled aloud after hanging up the phone ( ) This was his dream come true ( ) He could hardly wait for next Sunday to come ( )

2. When the Giants first snapped the ball, the crowd roared ( ) In truth, he had never even imagined anything could be so loud ( )

3. "He thought it was awesome, " Ty declared ( ) "He's looked like this for the last two hours ( ) First-timers tend to look like this ( ) But, don't worry ( ) He'll probably come back down to earth in time for school tomorrow ( )"

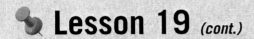

Name _____ Date _____

 ## Fluency Checkpoint

You have already listened to, practiced, and read the story below. Now it's time to check your reading fluency. Remember, fluency means not just getting the words right, but also reading at a good rate and with expression, or feeling. Reread the story again, as if you were rehearsing it for a performance. Repeat this as many times as necessary so that you can read it fluently.

Danny had always been a huge football fan. As soon as the fall schedule was announced, Danny marked on his calendar all the big games he wanted to watch. This year the New York Giants, his favorite team, were going to host their fierce and hated rivals—the Dallas Cowboys—the second week of October. Danny knew it was impossible, but he dreamed of being able to go to the game.

Then, one evening early in October, the phone rang. It was Danny's Uncle Alex. After a brief conversation about school and stuff, Uncle Alex said something that stunned Danny. Somehow Uncle Alex had gotten three tickets to the Dallas game and was inviting Danny to go to the game with him and his cousin, Ty. "Yahoo!" Danny yelled aloud after hanging up the phone. This was his dream come true! He could hardly wait for next Sunday to come!

The remainder of the week passed slowly and Danny had trouble being patient. But, finally Sunday arrived. Uncle Alex and Ty picked Danny up early. They had packed some sandwiches and drinks because they knew they would have to spend a couple of hours in the parking lot before getting in. Danny's heart skipped a beat when he saw the big welcome sign in front of Giants' Stadium.

The stadium was enormous. Most people were wearing red and blue, but there were a few Dallas fans scattered around. When the Giants first snapped the ball, the crowd roared. In truth, Danny had never even imagined anything could be so loud!

Danny watched the game and had the time of his life. When Uncle Alex brought him back home late in the afternoon, Danny's mom asked how it was. However, Danny just stood there, speechless. His eyes beamed but no words came out. Finally, Ty answered for him. "He thought it was awesome," Ty declared. "He's looked like this for the last two hours. First-timers tend to look like this. But, don't worry. He'll probably come back down to earth in time for school tomorrow!"

Evaluation

You are on your way to becoming a fluent reader! Evaluate your own progress by underlining true or false after each statement below.

1. My rate of reading (speed) is improving with practice.	true	false
2. When I read, I chunk words into phrases.	true	false
3. I pay attention to punctuation marks while I read.	true	false
4. I understand what it means to read with expression.	true	false

Name _____ Date _____

Phrases

Read these phrases to yourself as you listen to them being read aloud.

soft <u>glow</u> of lit candles	up to <u>thirty</u> children	lab coats are <u>worn</u>
on <u>duty</u>	<u>transported</u> here	<u>arithmetic</u> and <u>integers</u>
learning the <u>alphabet</u>	<u>attending</u> to everyone	<u>attending</u> a service
an <u>attendant</u> carries	<u>happening</u> all at once	some are <u>calm</u>
a tray of <u>juice</u>	of <u>religion</u>	with a tall <u>steeple</u>
<u>cheering</u> up the patients	<u>tonight</u> a man was	in perfect <u>harmony</u>
<u>carved</u> statues of figures	an <u>apartment</u> building	in a car <u>crash</u>
a <u>grand</u> hall	having <u>difficulty</u>	

Could you read every word? If not, repeat reading and listening until you can. Then, try reading the phrases on your own without listening.

Descriptions

Read the descriptions to yourself as you listen to them being read aloud. Then repeat reading and listening until you know every word. Try to figure out what is being described.

1. I am in a building that has many rooms. There is an office by the entrance. In most rooms there are **up to thirty children**. In one room, little children are **learning the alphabet**. In another room, children are working on math—**arithmetic and integers**. Where am I?

2. I am in a building where many things are **happening all at once**. Uniforms or **lab coats are worn** by almost everyone. In each room there are one or sometimes two people. **Some are calm.** Others are not. A woman is **having difficulty** breathing. **Tonight a man was in a car crash.** He was **transported here** by ambulance. Doctors and nurses are busy **attending to everyone** and **cheering up the patients** and families. Where am I?

3. I am in a building **with a tall steeple**. Inside is **a grand hall**. There is the **soft glow of lit candles**. People are **attending a service**. There are **carved statues of figures** and other symbols **of religion**. A choir sings **in perfect harmony**. Where am I?

4. I am in the lobby of a building with many floors. It looks something like **an apartment building**, but no one lives here. There is a man **on duty** at the front desk. People with suitcases come in and out. **An attendant carries a tray of juice** into the elevator. Someone must have ordered room service. Where am I?

Name _____ Date _____

On Your Own

You have listened to and read the descriptions of the various buildings. Now, reread each numbered description on page 89. Then, from the choices below, write the correct answer for each description.

| in an apartment | in a museum | in a school | in a store | in a library |
| in a hotel | in a hospital | in an office | in a church | in a restaurant |

1. _____
2. _____
3. _____
4. _____

Description Questions

Main Idea, Fact and Opinion, Vocabulary, Critical Thinking

Think about the descriptions you listened to and practiced on page 89. Now, find out how well you understood them! Answer the questions below. You may need to go back and read them again.

1. What is the main purpose of the reading activity in this lesson?
   A. To use word clues to figure out what is being described
   B. To describe five buildings
   C. To learn about different buildings
   D. To see if you were tricked by the extra answers

2. Which of these phrases provides the best clue for figuring out the specific place?
   A. I am in a building with many rooms.
   B. Inside is a grand hall.
   C. He was transported here by ambulance.
   D. There are carved statues of figures.

3. What could be the meaning of the word *steeple* in description 3?
   A. a church tower   C. Both A and B
   B. a pointed structure on a roof   D. Neither A nor B.

4. Choose one of the places listed in the "On Your Own" section that was not described. Write a short description in the style of the other descriptions. Use words and phrases that will give readers clues, but don't say what you are describing. End your description with "Where am I?"

   _____

   _____

   _____

                      © Shell Education

Name _____ Date _____

 # Reading with Expression—Auto-Correct (Proofreading)

By now, you are beginning to read well. Chances are that you are doing some things automatically. Your brain has learned to read many words on sight and to use punctuation clues to help you figure out where to stop, start, and pause. You are probably better at this than you realize. Let's find out!

Try It!

Read each description below. Tell your brain to be on the lookout for mistakes. See how many mistakes you can find. There might be missing or wrong punctuation marks, misspelled words, or incorrect capitalization. Highlight or circle the errors in a light color, such as yellow, pink, or orange.

1. I am in a building where many things are happening all at once Uniforms or lab coatz are worn by almost everyone. In each room there are one or sometimes two people. Some are calm! Others are not. A women is having difficulty breatheing. tonight a man was in a car crash. He was transportated here by ambulance. doctors and nurses are busy attending to everyone and cheering up the patients and families Where am I

2. I am in a building with a tall steepel. Inside is a grand hall! There is the soft glow of lit candles People are attending a Service. There are craved statues of figures and other cymbals of religion. a choir sings in perfect harmony. Where am I!

3. I am in the lobby of a building with meny floors? It looks sumthing like an apartment building, but no one lives here. Their is a man on duty at the front desk. People with suitcases come in and out? An attendant carries a tra of juice inta the elevator, Someone must have ordered room service. where am I?

Now, you should be ready to put your brain on "Auto-Correct." In other words, it should automatically be able to spot mistakes in capitalization, punctuation, and spelling— especially ones that were made accidentally. Go back to the description you wrote at the bottom of page 90. Proofread it. Then, rewrite it below without mistakes. Finally, trade papers with a partner to double check each other's work—just in case you missed something. Have your proofreader write his or initials in the box.

Proofread by

_____

_____

_____

_____

_____

Lesson 20 *(cont.)*

Name _____ Date _____

Fluency Checkpoint

You have already listened to, practiced, and read the descriptions below. Now it's time to check your reading fluency. Remember, fluency means not just getting the words right, but also reading at a good rate and with expression, or feeling. Reread the descriptions again, as if you were rehearsing it for a performance. Repeat this as many times as necessary so that you can read it fluently.

1. I am in a building that has many rooms. There is an office by the entrance. In most rooms there are up to thirty children. In one room, little children are learning the alphabet. In another room, children are working on math—arithmetic and integers. Where am I? (I am in a school.)

2. I am in a building where many things are happening all at once. Uniforms or lab coats are worn by almost everyone. In each room there are one or sometimes two people. Some are calm. Others are not. A woman is having difficulty breathing. Tonight a man was in a car crash. He was transported here by ambulance. Doctors and nurses are busy attending to everyone and cheering up the patients and families. Where am I? (I am in a hospital.)

3. I am in a building with a tall steeple. Inside is a grand hall. There is the soft glow of lit candles. People are attending a service. There are carved statues of figures and other symbols of religion. A choir sings in perfect harmony. Where am I? (I am in a church.)

4. I am in the lobby of a building with many floors. It looks something like an apartment building, but no one lives here. There is a man on duty at the front desk. People with suitcases come in and out. An attendant carries a tray of juice into the elevator. Someone must have ordered room service. Where am I? (I am in a hotel.)

Evaluation

Do you think teachers give out grades on report cards? Actually, they just *record* the grades that *you* have earned. It's the end of the year and here is a "Fluency Report Card." On each line, fill in *A, B, C, D,* or *F*— the grade that you think you have earned in each category.

My Fluency Report Card

	Accuracy	Rate (Speed)	Expression
1. Reading Skill	_____	_____	_____
2. Improvement	_____	_____	_____
3. Effort	_____	_____	_____

Overall Fluency Grade _____

#50279—*Increasing Fluency with High Frequency Word Phrases*   © *Shell Education*

Answer Key

Lesson 1

On Your Own (page 14)
1. tall-tale characters
2. from the Atlantic to the Pacific
3. in Texas
4. paid his dues

Story Questions (page 14)
1. D
2. B
3. A
4. Answers will vary.

Try It! (page 15)
1. horns, which
2. 1870s, a man
3. concerned, Old Blue
4. longhorn, Old Blue
5. ranch, pampered

Lesson 2

On Your Own (page 18)
1. in Egypt
2. a young fellow
3. whispered to myself
4. through the dust

Story Questions (page 18)
1. B
2. 2, 4, 1, 5, 3,
3. D
4. Answers will vary.

Try It! (page 19)
1. B
2. B
3. A

Lesson 3

On Your Own (page 22)
Sentences will vary.

Story Questions (page 22)
1. C
2. A
3. a material made of hydrogen and carbon; it floats in water
4. A

Try It! (page 23)
1. here
2. prevent
3. something

Lesson 4

On Your Own (page 26)
1. artist
2. powerful
3. scene
4. rough
5. standard

Story Questions (page 26)
1. D
2. D
3. B
4. Answers will vary.

Try It! (page 27)
1. bored; slow, low
2. light-hearted; quicker, higher
3. painful; slow, low

Lesson 5

On Your Own (page 30)
1. kids; have
2. relative; could push
3. force; accept
4. heroes; expect to start
5. I; have

Story Questions (page 30)
1. A
2. A
3. B
4. Answers will vary.

Try It! (page 31)
1. inform
2. persuade
3. entertain

Lesson 6

On Your Own (page 34)
Answers will vary.

Story Questions (page 34)
1. A
2. B
3. D
4. Answers will vary.

Try It! (page 35)
Answers will vary.

Lesson 7

On Your Own (page 38)
Writing will vary.

Editorial Questions (page 38)
1. C
2. D
3. A
4. Answers will vary.

Lesson 8

On Your Own (page 42)
Writing will vary.

8	1	6
3	5	7
4	9	2

Letter Questions (page 42)
1. D
2. B
3. B
4–5. Answers will vary.

Answer Key *(cont.)*

Try It! (page 43)
1. <u>She'd</u> sit there . . . <u>they</u> got . . . <u>they</u> were . . . <u>she'd</u> have it
2. <u>she</u> only . . . <u>her</u> dad . . . showed <u>her</u>

Lesson 9

On Your Own (page 46)
Sentences will vary.

Story Questions (page 46)
1. C
2. 3, 2, 4, 1
3. D
4. Germany, Japan

Try It! (page 47)
Possible Chunking:

It was the fifth year of the war / Nothing prevented the United States / from picking up the enemy's messages / but they were in code / In theory / any code has a rational pattern / It should be just a matter of figuring it out / Dozens of the best minds at the time / were put to the task / of breaking the code / Yet they struggled / Some believed that Germany had finally invented / a code that couldn't be broken.

Evaluation (page 48)
1. A
2. B

Lesson 10

On Your Own (page 50)
Writing will vary.

Story Questions (page 50)
1. D
2. B and C
3. A

4. Questions copied from the story: Why . . . ? If . . . ?
5. Answers will vary.

Try It! (page 51)
1. (?) going up
2. (!)(!) rising and ending sharply
3. (?) going up

Lesson 11

On Your Own (page 54)
Answers will vary.

Story Questions (page 54)
1. C
2. D
3. D
4. C

Try It! (page 55)
1. he found her at a ball.
2. he spotted her in a tall tower and climbed her long hair.
3. "How about sliding that dish my way?"

Lesson 12

On Your Own (page 58)
Words underlined. (Either whole words or accented syllables.)
<u>this</u>, <u>there</u>, <u>three</u>
<u>follow</u>, <u>on</u>, <u>line</u>
<u>notice</u>, <u>there's</u>, <u>pattern</u>
<u>Of</u>, <u>lines</u>, <u>rhyme</u>
1. three matching stressed beats in each line
2. the same

Poem Questions (page 58)
1. B
2. C
3. boat (or ship)

Try It! (page 59)
stressed syllables: just, dog, crew/ two, us, go/ lo, sloop, Sue/ knew, route, go/ map, clear, la/ how, wind, blow/ hur, to, bay/ fas, up, sails/ we, on, way/ sail, way, last/ land, way, hind/ sud, ly, gasp

Lesson 13

On Your Own (page 62)
1. to take kids.
2. a blend of adventure and history.
3. Native American life.
4. alive and personal.
5. societies of long ago.

Review Questions (page 62)
1. A
2. C
3. D
4. Answers will vary.

Try It! (page 63)
1. museum
2. scene or seen
3. societies
4. soldiers
5. frequently
6. eager
7. reflected
8. conclusion

© Shell Education